KNITTING CRASH COURSE

The Ultimate Beginner's Course to Learning How to Knit In Under 12 Hours - *Including Quick Projects & Detailed Images*

By Elizabeth Hamilton

Table of Contents

INTRODUCTION: WELCOME TO YOUR NEW FAVORITE HOBBY! 6

CHAPTER 1: THE ABCS OF KNITTING 8

    BASIC SUPPLIES YOU WILL NEED TO START KNITTING 8
    CHOOSING YARN 9
    CHOOSING KNITTING NEEDLES 10
    STITCH MARKERS 13
    YARN NEEDLES 13
    A WAY TO COUNT ROWS 13
    CROCHET HOOK 14

CHAPTER 2: GETTING STARTED 15

    MAKE A YARN BALL 15
    CASTING ON 16
    THE TWO DIFFERENT TYPES OF KNITTING 20

CHAPTER 3: YOUR FIRST STICH 22

    KNIT STITCH 22
    TROUBLESHOOTING 25
    DROPPED STITCHES: WHAT THEY ARE AND HOW TO CORRECT THEM 25

CHAPTER 4: YOUR FIRST PROJECT: THE HANDMADE DISHCLOTH 29

    BASIC INSTRUCTIONS 29
    BINDING OFF IN KNITTING 30
    WEAVING IN YOUR ENDS 31

CHAPTER 5: YOUR SECOND PROJECT: THE EASY HAT IN THE ROUND 34

    BASIC INSTRUCTIONS 35
    CASTING ON IN THE ROUND 35
    JOINING IN THE ROUND 36
    KNIT 2 TOGETHER 37
    FINISHING THE EASY HAT IN THE ROUND 38

CHAPTER 6: YOUR THIRD PROJECT: THE TEXTURED SCARF 39

- The Purl Stitch 39
- Troubleshooting 40
- Basic Instructions 41
- Introducing a New Ball of Yarn 41

CHAPTER 7: NOW YOU'RE KNITTING! 43

- A Selection of Common Stitch Patterns 43
- Adding Stripes of Color to Your Work 45
- Jog-less Color Change While Knitting in the Round 46
- Basic Knitting Abbreviations 48
- Reading a Written Knitting Pattern 49
- Gauge Swatches: What Are They and How To Make Them 52

CHAPTER 8: BLOCKING YOUR WORK 55

- Wet Blocking 56
- Spray or Spritz Blocking 58
- Steam Blocking 58

CHAPTER 9: YOUR FOURTH PROJECT: THE CABLED HEADBAND 60

- The Pattern 60
- Making Cables 62
- Joining Edges Together 63

CHAPTER 10: YOUR FIFTH PROJECT: A DISHCLOTH ON THE BIAS 64

- The Pattern 64
- Knitting on the Bias 64
- Yarn Over 65

CHAPTER 11: A COLLECTION OF PROJECTS TO KEEP YOU GOING 67

- Yarn Over Shawl With Drop Stitch Detail 67
- Elongated Stitch Scarf 68
- Double Pattern Cowl 70
- Quick Leg Warmers 70
- Luxury Cowl 72

EYELET SCARF 72
CABLE SCARF 73

CHAPTER 12: BONUS & CONCLUSION 75

HINTS, TIPS, AND REMINDERS 75
IN CLOSING 76

PREVIEW OF CROCHET CRASH COURSE - THE ULTIMATE BEGINNER'S COURSE TO LEARNING HOW TO CROCHET IN UNDER 12 HOURS - *INCLUDING QUICK PROJECTS & DETAILED IMAGES* 78

ABOUT THE AUTHOR 85

© Copyright 2015

All rights reserved. No portion of this book may be reproduced - mechanically, electronically, or by any other means, including photocopying- without the permission of the publisher.

Disclaimer

The information provided in this book is designed to provide helpful information on the subjects discussed. The author's books are only meant to provide the reader with the basics knowledge of knitting, without any warranties regarding whether the student will, or will not, be able to incorporate and apply all the information provided. Although the writer will make her best effort share her insights. This book, nor any of the author's books constitute a promise that the reader will learn a knitting within a certain timeframe. The illustrations are guidance.

Introduction:
Welcome to Your New Favorite Hobby!

So, you've decided to learn how to knit? Well, congratulations and welcome to your new favorite hobby! You're going to love it! Knitting can be a great way for you to relax while still actually being productive. It can also be an affordable way for you to make expensive-looking clothing items and gifts without having to spend a fortune. With this guide, in a very short time, you will be able to knit on your own and to take pride in having crafted beautiful creations with your own hands, while you and your loved ones enjoy the fruits of your not-so-laborious labor.

Learning how to do something is wonderful, but actually crafting something useful *while* you're learning, well that's even better. This guide is designed to allow you to do that. You'll learn a few basics, and then use them to create a piece. Then, you'll learn a couple of new techniques and use them to create another piece. As you keep adding to your knitting skill-set, you will keep adding to your collection of beautiful and useful completed works. With this guide, you will learn knitting terminology and techniques as you are gaining practical, real-life knitting knowledge and experience. What better way to learn?

Meant both as a step-by-step introduction to knitting and as a reference tool, this guide will help you get your foot on the ladder and hopefully avoid most of the usual beginner's mistakes.

Get ready to impress yourself and others with your newfound craftiness in the realm of needle arts!

Let's get started!

Elizabeth Hamilton

Chapter 1
The ABCs of Knitting

Basic Supplies You Will Need to Start Knitting

Unless you already have knitting supplies at your disposal, you will need to make a quick store run or put in an online order for a few things to get started. You can find these basic supplies at any craft store and at most discount stores and superstores that have any sort of craft section.

To begin, you will need:

• Yarn

Something in a medium or worsted weight (4 or 5) for our purposes, choose the skeins of yarn so that each project is in a solid color of your choice; 1 skein for The Handmade Dish Cloth; 1 additional skein for The Easy Hat; and 2 additional skeins for The Patterned Scarf

• Knitting Needles

One Pair of 9" Straight Needles Size U.S. 11 / 8.0mm
One Pair of 16" Circular Needles Size U.S. 11 / 8.0mm

• Stitch Markers

It's best to have more than one color available; the cheap plastic ones work just fine

• Yarn Needles

These look like overgrown sewing needles; they can usually be found made from plastic or from metal

• A Way to Count Rows

You can buy any kind of counting device at a craft store or online, or you can simply make hash marks with a pencil and paper; either method will work

• Crochet Hook

A small to mid-sized U.S. 3 / 3.25mm – U.S. 5 / 3.75mm crochet hook; they can be found made from varying materials; a cheap plastic one will suffice

• Scissors

You didn't really think that there would be an explanation here for scissors, did you?

Choosing Yarn

You will find that there is a vast array of yarn available out there. Yarns of different weights (determined by the thickness of the strands), made from a whole host of different materials, in just about every color imaginable. There is no need to be intimidated by the selection, though! With just a little common sense and a bit of forethought, you can allow your creativity to take the reigns and steer your choice of yarn in the direction that works best for your project and your budget.

For your first adventure in knitting, there is no need to spend a fortune on fancy yarn. It is much more important that you choose a yarn suitable for your project. For instance, the yarn you want to use for The Adorable

Dishcloth, which will be the first project you make with this guide, should be one that is made from a sturdy material that will not shrink in warm water; an acrylic or acrylic blend would work wonderfully. Whereas, for The Textured Scarf and The Easy Hat, your second and third projects, you are going to want a yarn that is softer on the skin and maybe even washable, like a cotton or a wool blend. So, be sure to take into consideration what you are creating and its intended use when making your yarn choice.

Many patterns will give you a specific weight of yarn to use. Most yarns that are commercially sold have a guide table on the label that lets you know the weight of the yarn and what knitting needle size is recommended for the best results. They make it so easy for us!

Choosing Knitting Needles

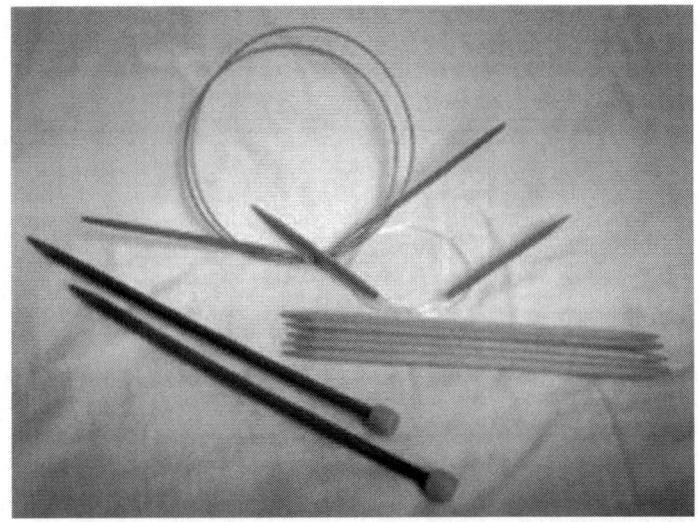

Once you have made your yarn selection, choosing your knitting needles will be relatively easy. Keep in mind that there are straight needles, circular needles, and double pointed needles. For the beginner and into the intermediate areas of knitting, you will only need to be familiar with the straight needles and the circular needles, but for the sake of intimately getting to know your craft, we will touch on double pointed needles as well.

Straight needles are exactly that: straight. They are made from a variety of different materials including metal, wood, and plastic; and can be found in varying lengths to suit whatever project you can imagine. Straight needles will always have some sort of knob on the end opposite the point. They generally range in size from U.S. 0 (2mm) to U.S. 15 (10mm) and range in length from 10in (25cm) to 16in (40cm). Straight knitting needles are designed to knit only flat pieces of fabric.

Circular knitting needles are two short needles joined together by a flexible cord to form one continuous needle. They can be used to knit flat projects or projects knit in the round. Like straight needles, they can be found made from many different materials. The sizes of the circular needles are the same as straight needles, but the lengths are different. You can find them in lengths ranging from 16in (40cm) to 40in (101cm) and beyond. Circular knitting needles can be used to knit both flat pieces and pieces "in the round". Knitting in the round produces a tube of fabric.

When considering circular needles, it is important to make sure that the cord joining the two short needles is smooth so that it will not catch or fray your yarn. I recommend circular needles with nylon cords.

Double pointed needles have a point at each end just like their name implies. Their double points make it possible for the knitter to knit off of either end of the needle. They are usually sold in sets of four or five and allow for projects to be knit in the round without circular needles. There is one distinct advantage to using double pointed knitting needles in place of circular knitting needles to knit in the round. This advantage lies in the fact that because the cord on the circular needles can only be so short and still allow for the points to come together to knit, circular knitting needles are not an effective tool to use for knitting very, very small works in the round, like tiny baby socks. Their double pointed counterparts, however, are quite well suited for these types of purposes since one can knit off of either end. Double pointed knitting needles, like their straight and circular relatives, can also be found in a range of lengths and materials, but are traditionally made from some kind of wood. They are available in the same standard knitting needle sizes as are straight and circular knitting needles.

Just about all commercially manufactured knitting needles, whether they are straight, circular, or double pointed, are marked on either the knobs opposite their points or on the needles themselves with their size, generally in the standard U.S. size, as well as the metric size. The size of a knitting needle refers to its circumference.

Choosing the type and size knitting needles to be used is generally dictated by the type of piece one will knit and the size of the yarn used to knit said piece, respectively. The choice of material from which the knitting needles are made, is almost always a knitter's personal preference. Some knitters like the subtle clinking sound produced by metal knitting needles while others prefer the feel of the wooden knitting needles in their hands. I will tell you what no one told me when I was a beginner knitter: It is not advisable as a beginner to start off knitting on metal knitting needles unless they are the only needles available to you. The yarn slides around on them very easily, which is great once you have gotten the hang of knitting. In fact, eventually, it can even help you to knit faster. But, all that yarn sliding around so easily on the knitting needles means that the yarn can easily slide *off* the knitting needles, too, and that is not going to be helpful to you at this point.

So, I strongly suggest that until you are at least two or three projects in to this whole knitting thing, you use wooden knitting needles. Generally they tend to create just a bit more friction between themselves and the yarn so there is less likelihood of your precious stitches accidentally dropping off of them. They can be found made out of just about any and every wood imaginable, but again, there is no need to run out and spend a fortune on mahogany (yes, those actually do exist) or some other super-fancy needles. A nice set of pine or bamboo knitting needles will do just fine.

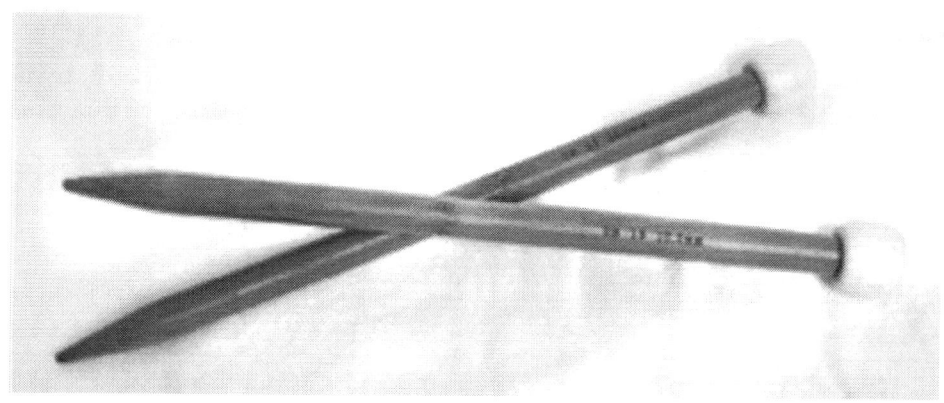

Stitch Markers

Before I started knitting, I had no idea what these were or what their intended purpose was. As a knitter who now does a lot of knitting in the round and pattern work, I can tell you that these little guys are invaluable! They are used to mark specific spots in your knitting, and more specifically, a certain number of stitches. Try to knit in the round or do some pattern work and without them, and you will have to spend a lot of time counting stitches to keep your place, and at the risk of miscounting or losing count. Trust me; get them. You'll see what I mean!

Yarn Needles

Yarn needles (sometimes called darning needles) are not the same as knitting needles. These needles look like the older, but much duller, big brother of sewing needles and you will need them to weave in the ends or tails of your yarn that are left hanging after your knitting work is done. Weaving in your ends is a finishing step to just about every project you will ever do as a knitter and a very important means of keeping your precious creations from unraveling. I like to use the metal yarn needles since they do not get bent and thus, do not need to be replaced as often, but the plastic ones work well, too.

A Way to Count Rows

There are many different types of counting devices available. There are manual counters that add by turning a dial and those that can be clicked to count. There are digital counters that count with the touch of a button. Some counting devices are even designed to slip onto a knitting needle and can pull double duty as a stitch marker, too! It does not really matter what is used to keep track of your row count. You can use a pencil and paper and count with hash marks if you like. It is only important that your row count is kept consistently and accurately. This is especially true once you start using different stitches to create patterns in your work.

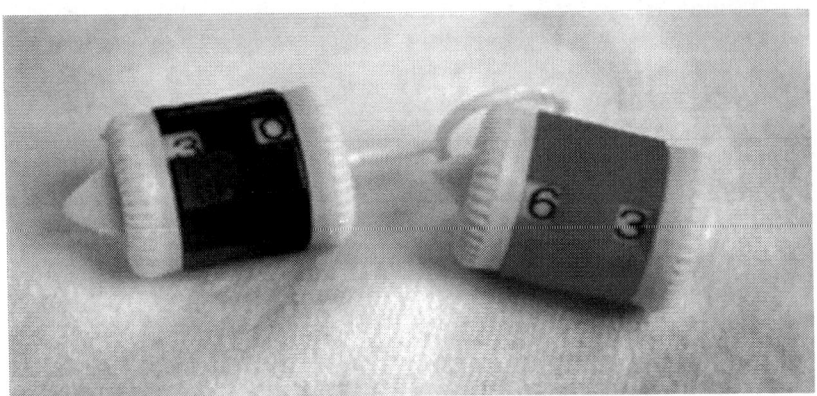

Crochet Hook

Yes, this is still your knitting guide; and don't worry, we will not be going over crochet techniques. It just so happens that this handy little hook is perfect for correcting one of the most common of all knitting mistakes, so it is advisable to keep one near.

Crochet hooks, of course, come in different sizes and are made from a variety of materials. For knitters, all that is needed is an inexpensive, small to mid-sized crochet hook. If it seems odd, that your knitting guide is suggesting that you purchase a crochet hook, please, have faith. You will be glad you did!

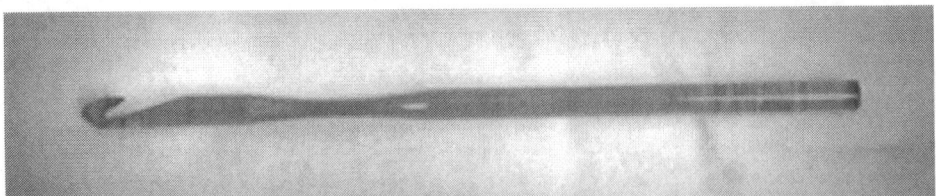

14

Chapter 2:
Getting Started

So, now you have gathered your supplies, and are ready to get to the good part: knitting! You have just one more quick step before you move on!

Make A Yarn Ball

Making a yarn ball from a skein of yarn is strongly suggested. Now, I know you're probably thinking, "I just bought this yarn and here it is, wound up all nicely and neatly! Why would I want to spend my precious knitting time rewinding it into a silly ball?" I'll tell you why.

Because of the way the yarn is twisted as it is wound up by a machine during manufacturing, if you knit directly from the skeins or hanks of yarn that you buy at the store, your yarn will eventually tangle up on you while you are knitting. This can be pretty frustrating when you are right in the middle of a project. So, though it is not an absolutely crucial step, I do highly recommend taking a few minutes to do it.

Just find the end of your yarn and loosely wrap it 10 or 12 times around two fingers. Slip the wrapped yarn off your fingers and start wrapping around that. You'll get the hang of it quickly. Turn your ball after every six or seven wraps for evenness of appearance. Keep doing this, and in a few minutes, you will have a cute little ball of yarn that will not tangle up on you while you are working your knitting magic.

If at anytime in your knitting adventures, winding your yarn into a ball becomes too tedious a task for you, take heart. There are simple machines available for purchase, which are designed to wind yarn into a ball. They are called Ball Winders or Yarn Ball Machines. Many stores, like specialty yarn shops and knitting supply stores that specifically cater to those of us who knit and/or crochet, are equipped with these machines for patrons to use. Sometimes, if the store clerks are very nice, they will even offer to wind your yarn for you.

Casting On

Casting on is the means of getting the yarn onto your knitting needle to start a project. It creates a row of loops around the needle and each loop counts as a stitch in your first row.

You will need one straight knitting needle and your ball of yarn. Measure out about one arm's length of yarn off the ball. To make it easier, keep the ball of yarn on your left with the end, or tail, of the yarn to your right. The first thing to do when making your cast on row is to make a slipknot. There are many different ways to do this, but I'm going to teach you the easiest way that I have found.

Loosely loop the yarn around the index and middle finger of your left hand. Slip the loop off your fingers. Lay the loop flat in your left hand so that the tail end of the yarn is trailing off to the right and it cuts across the circle. Grab your needle with your right hand. Pick up the strand of yarn that's cutting across your loop by sliding your needle underneath it and scooping it up. With your left hand, grab both the tail end and the working end of your yarn and gently pull them apart to tighten the knot around your knitting needle. Be careful not to tighten your knot too much. You want it snug on the needle, but not actually tight. If it is too tight, it will be difficult to knit through on the next row. You should be able to slide your other knitting needle through the loop that is on the first needle without having to force it.

Keep your first finger on the loop to keep it from sliding off your needle. When you hold your knitting needle up and look at your slipknot, the working end of the yarn (the yarn attached to the ball) should be in the front and the tail end should be in the back. If you see that it's the other way around, simply slide your slipknot off your needle, turn it around, and put it back on your needle.

With both strands hanging down properly, insert your left thumb and forefinger between them. Then make your left hand into a gun shape, opening the strands up so that the working end of the yarn wraps around your extended thumb while the tail end wraps around your extended forefinger. Grasp both ends loosely in your remaining three fingers.

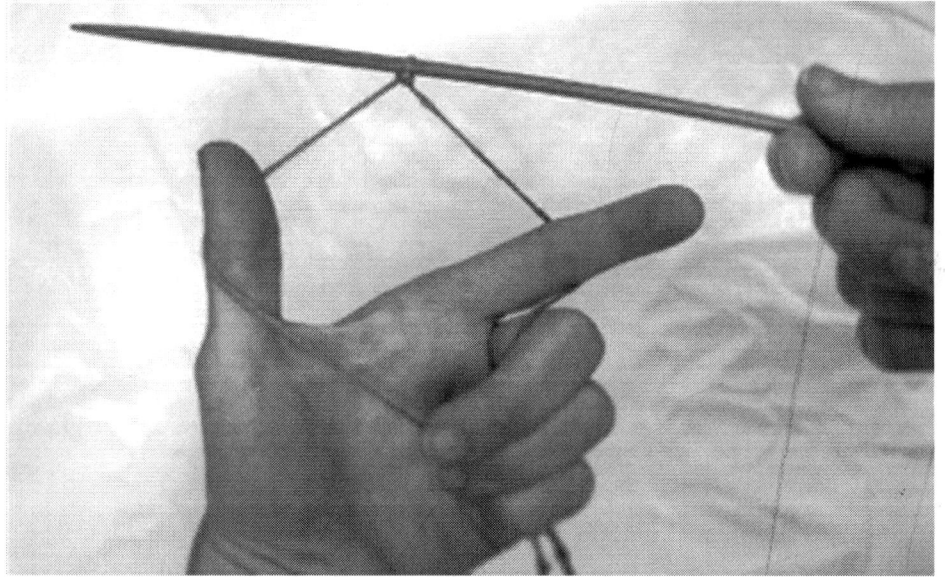

Bring down the tip of your needle and catch the strand of yarn that is on your thumb by scooping up from under it.

17

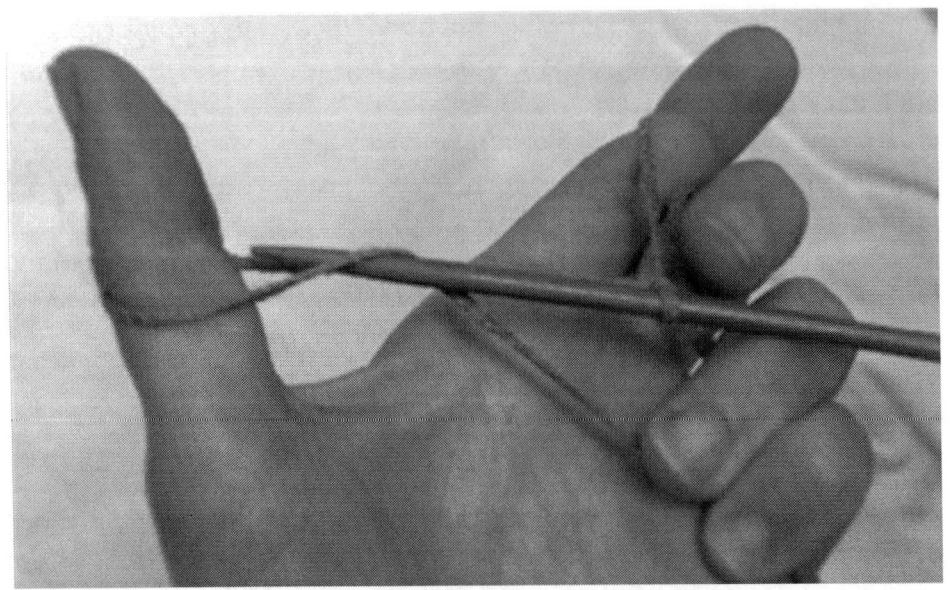

Then, take the tip of your needle up to your forefinger and catch the strand of yarn that is around it by scooping it from above.

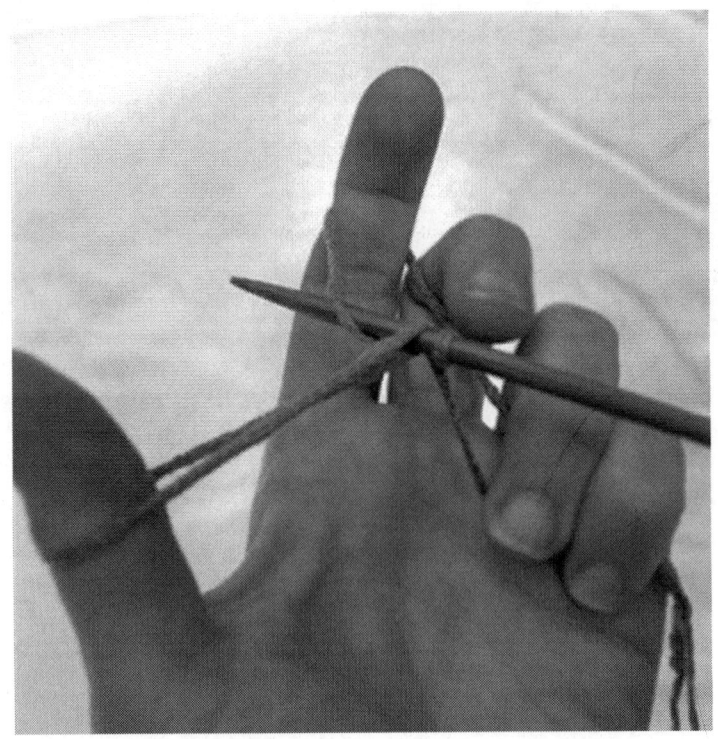

Next, take the tip of your needle back through the yarn around your thumb. You will notice that you are sort of exiting back through the yarn

18

looped around your thumb. You just need to release the yarn from around your thumb and tighten up what is now (Voila!) the second stitch on your cast on row.

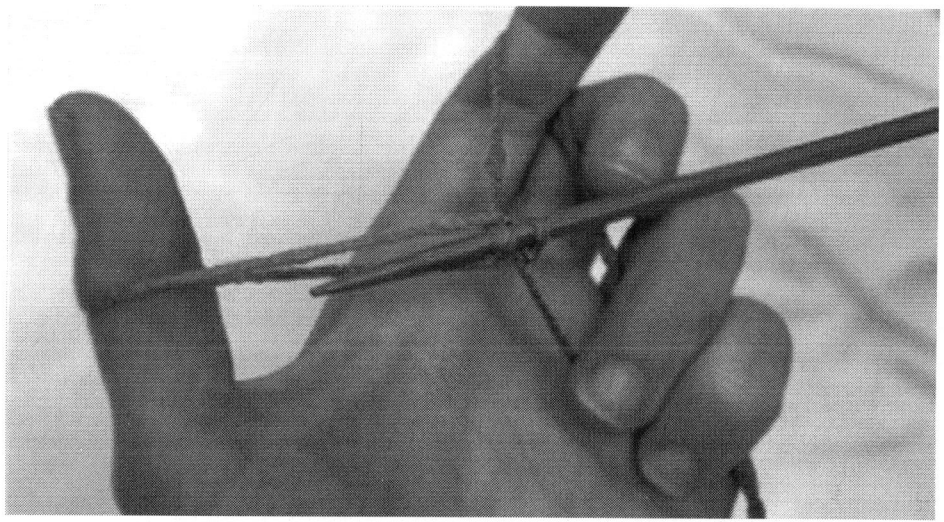

Go ahead and repeat this process until you have about 20 loops on your needle. Remember that each loop is one stitch. In order for you to become proficient and consistent, I highly recommend that you practice making your cast on row several times before moving on to the next section. To start from scratch, simply pull your stitches off of your knitting needle and pull both of the yarn strands to unravel it all. This type of purposeful unraveling is called "ripping back". After you have ripped back your cast on row, slide your slipknot off of the needle and pull both ends of your yarn to make the knot disappear. It's like it never even existed! But, now that you have created a cast on row, you can do it again and again; and it will get easier each time! Remember to practice keeping the stitches snug, not tight!

The Two Different Types of Knitting

Before we jump into the knit stitch, there are a couple of quick points that I would like to cover. The purpose in mentioning these points is simply to increase your knowledge about knitting which can help you later when communicating with other knitters.

There are actually two types of knitting. The types are specific to with which hand one holds the working yarn.

If the knitter works the yarn off of their right hand, it is called American or English knitting, and the yarn is "thrown" over the knitting needle to make the stitch. If the yarn is worked off of the knitter's left hand, it is called Continental knitting or picking, and the left index finger is used to assist the needle in picking up the yarn to make the stitch.

Usually, when asked, whichever was the way a knitter first learned to knit, is the way that they will tell you is best. That being said, neither method is right or wrong. In fact, some knitters learn to be proficient in both types, but the Continental knitting method uses a considerably subtler movement of the hand and arm. For this reason, it is thought to be the faster and more efficient of the two methods. It is also considered to be much less of a problem for people who suffer from repetitive stress problems, like Carpal Tunnel Syndrome. Taking all of these factors into consideration, you will be learning the Continental knitting method from this guide.

Chapter 3
Our first Stich

Knit Stitch

Now that you have become comfortable making a cast on row, you are ready to learn your first stitch! It is the basis of all knitting from the very simplest piece to the most intricate and complex of patterns. I present to you, the Knit Stitch!

Go ahead and make a cast on row of 20 stitches (look at you go!). Now switch the needle with your cast on row to your left hand. Hold up your cast on row and examine it. The working end of the yarn should be coming off the back of your needle at this point and the tail end of the yarn should be coming off of the front. Your stitches should be similar in appearance. They should be pretty uniformly snug, but not tight on the needle with a little bit of room to allow for both needles to be in the same stitch at once without needing to resort to force. They should also all be facing the same way. Take note here that in knitting, each stitch is said to have two "legs". When a stitch is on the knitting needle, its legs come off the back and front of the needle. No matter which side of your knitted work is facing you, the left leg of a stitch is considered to be the back of the stitch and the right leg of a stitch is considered to be the front. After a thorough examination of your cast on row and maybe one more count of your stitches, it is time to experiment with different ways of holding your yarn.

Some people wrap the working end of their yarn around the left index finger and then weave it in between their other fingers to keep a good grip on it. Others just hold the yarn without weaving it in and out of their bottom three fingers and they let it come over the top of their index finger. This is another type of thing that is purely a personal preference of the knitter. So, try out a few different ways of holding on to your yarn and weaving it or not weaving it in and out of different fingers. Just remember that you will be holding the knitting needle and the working end of the yarn in your left hand. With your left index finger, you will need to provide a little bit of tension on the yarn by gently pulling it back and away from where it comes off of the needle, but not too much tension, otherwise as you knit and use more yarn, it will be difficult to steadily feed the yarn up to the knitting needles. Find a way to hold it that is relatively comfortable, keeping in mind that you can always change it later if you decide it just is not suiting you. If you do choose to wrap the yarn around your finger or fingers, take care to avoid doing so too tightly. Not only can that make it difficult for the yarn to be easily fed to your index finger to be worked into a stitch, but it can also result in poor circulation to your fingertips, and nobody wants that!

Now that you have chosen a satisfactory way to hold your yarn, you can commence with your knitting. Holding the needle that is hosting your cast on row in your left hand and your left index finger providing a little bit of gentle tension on the yarn, grab your other knitting needle in your right hand. This will be your working needle. Carefully insert the tip of the working needle from back to front (remember, in knitting language, that means from left to right!), through the loop closest to the point of your other needle so that both needles are now in the loop. Allow your working needle to go behind the other needle creating an X with the tips.

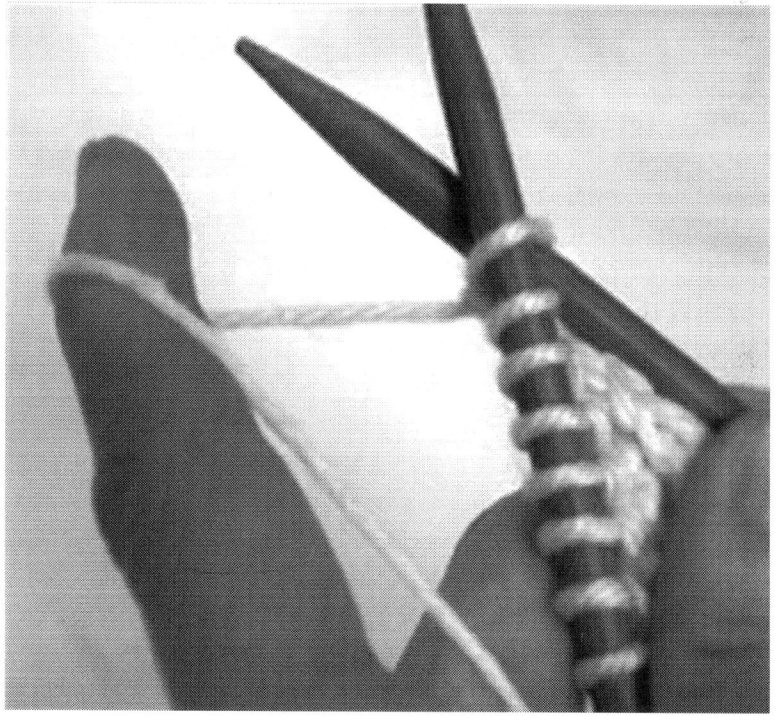

Use your index finger to wrap the yarn around the tip of the working needle from left to right.

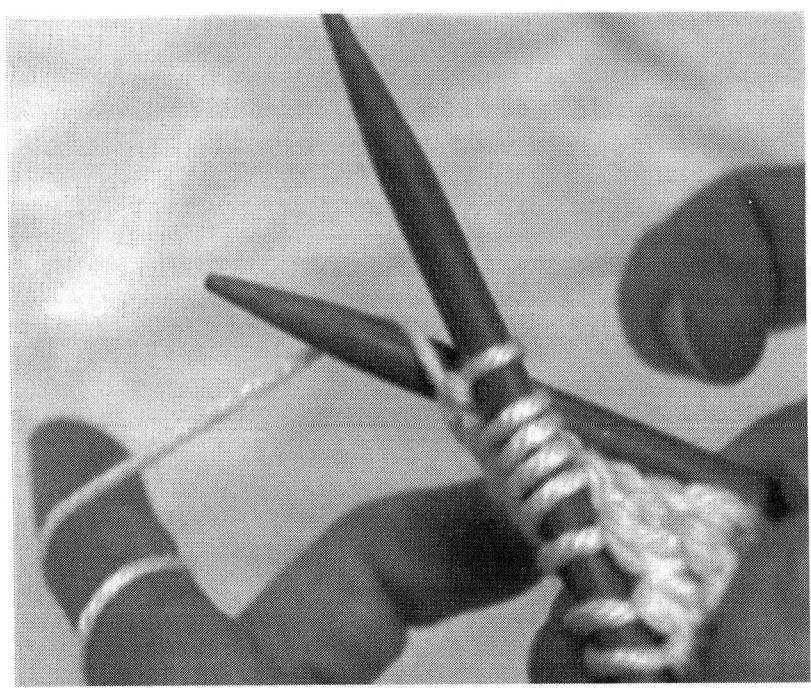

As you become more proficient (and it won't take long!), most of the motion needed to wrap the yarn will come from dipping the tip of your working needle down and picking up the yarn with the tip of that needle and less of the motion will be from your left index finger. Once the working yarn is around the end of the working needle, bring the tip of the needle back through the loop so that you are exiting the loop from your cast on row that you originally entered.

Slide that loop from your cast on row off of its needle. Notice that when you slide it off the needle, it makes a little loop around the base of the new stitch. Gently tighten the new stitch on your working needle by pulling your working yarn back and away from the knitting needle. Just like in creating your cast on row, you don't want to tighten it too much or it will be hard to work through on the next row.

Hooray! You just made your first Knit Stitch! You should now have one stitch on your working needle and nineteen stitches on your non-working needle. Repeat this process with each of the remaining nineteen stitches, taking care not to over-tighten any of the new stitches. After your first row has been worked and all of the new stitches are on your working needle, transfer that needle to your left hand and the empty needle will now become the working needle in your right hand.

Go ahead and knit 10 to 20 rows. Knit until you feel yourself getting more comfortable with the way you hold your yarn, the way you hold your needles, and the way you use the working needle to pick up the working yarn from your left index finger. Examine your stitches, both on the needles and in the fabric that you are creating. Familiarize yourself with how they are supposed to look.

Troubleshooting

If your stitches are getting twisted, it means that you are wrapping your yarn from right to left around your working needle instead of from left to right. If you end up with an extra stitch on your row, it means that you need to be sure and pull your working yarn to the back of your needle before knitting your next stitch. Because of this, it is advisable, at this point, for a beginner to count the stitches on the needle after each row. Counting the stitches will also help to catch dropped stitches before they run and before they are able to get away from you! What are dropped stitches, you ask?

Dropped Stitches: What They Are and How To Correct Them

If any of the loops slip off either needle, that loop is considered to be a dropped stitch. All knitters, regardless of their skill level, inevitably drop stitches. Sometimes you notice right away, and sometimes you might knit several rows before you notice. The important thing to remember is not to panic. Just deal with the problem as soon as possible. If a dropped stitch goes uncorrected, it will leave an unsightly "run" in your work and can ruin both the appearance as well as the viability of your piece. As you gain more experience you will be able to recognize them sooner than later and they won't make you feel like you are having a knitting crisis so much as just a minor inconvenience.

We are going to go over the correction of two degrees of dropped stitches: the dropped stitch with a short run, and the dropped stitch with a long run.

If the stitch has only dropped by one row, it is considered a "short run". This is pretty easy to correct, as long as you are able to keep from stretching open your fabric. If you are fortunate enough to see the dropped stitch right away, then just pick it up with the opposite needle and put it back on the needle from which it dropped. It is important to make sure that when you place it back on its needle, the stitch is facing the correct way. You can check it by comparing it to the other stitches. If it is twisted, simply slip it back onto the opposite needle and then correct its direction when you slip it back onto its own needle.

If a dropped stitch has either gone unnoticed for a couple of rows or has run itself down several rows, this is considered a "long run".

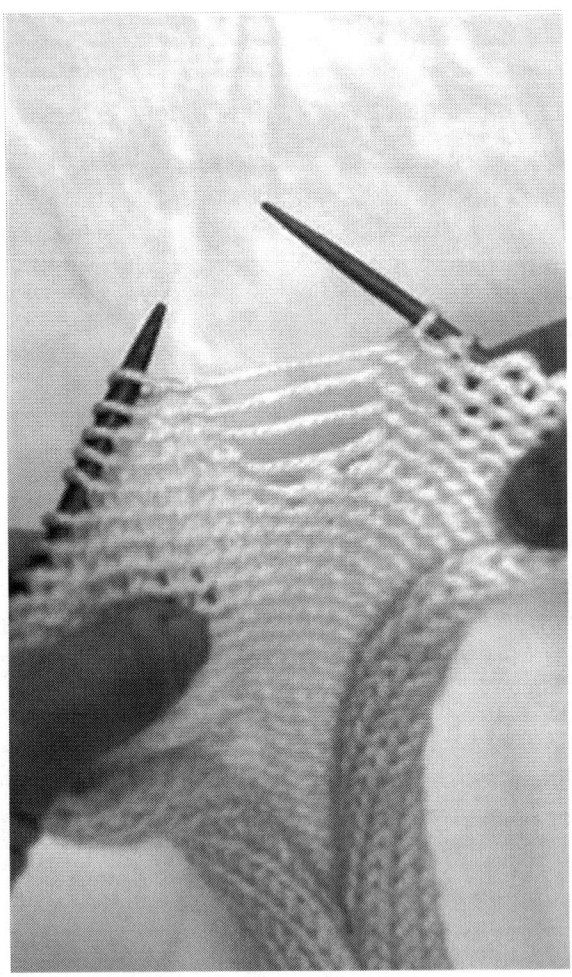

Remember not to panic! Everything will be fine in the "long run". Yes, that was a little knitting joke. Anyway, the first thing you want to do is grab that handy little crochet hook, because it is about to show you its worth! Insert the crochet hook into the dropped stitch from front to back being sure the hook has a hold of the stitch. Securing it now on the crochet hook will keep the run from getting any longer while you get ready to correct it. You will need to position the run from your dropped stitch directly between the points of your needles as if the dropped stitch were the one on which you are working. If on your current row you have not reached the location of the run, keep knitting until you get to it. If on your current row you have already passed the run, you will want to "slip" the stitches between your current working yarn stitch and the run.

To slip stitches, simply means to move the stitches from the needle that they are on to whichever needle that they are not on, without working them. So, in this case, you will slip each stitch from the working needle back onto the opposite needle until you reach the run.

Once you are in position, pick up the crochet hook that has been so dutifully holding the dropped stitch. You may want to carefully stretch out the run enough to get a good look at it. Gently push the crochet hook through the dropped stitch that it's holding just a little bit so that the hook is free to grab more yarn. Then, use the hook to grab the first horizontal bar of yarn above the dropped stitch. Pull that horizontal bar through the dropped stitch.

You just worked the horizontal bar of a run into a stitch! Continue working up by grabbing each successive horizontal bar and pulling it through the stitch on your crochet hook until there are no more bars. Once you have reached the top, slip the stitch from your crochet hook back to the knitting needle on which it belongs. If you need to slip some previously worked stitches back onto your working needle to get back to your proper place on the row, you can use the stitch from which your working yarn comes as your guide. When that stitch is the closest one to the point of your working needle, you are good to go and can pick right back up where you left off.

Chapter 4
Your First Project: The Handmade Dishcloth

So, you can now make a yarn ball, cast on a row of stitches, knit your little heart out, and even identify and correct dropped stitches without losing your cool! You, my friend, are ready for your first project!

This little dishcloth is quick and easy to knit, and will give you enough practice in each of the techniques you have learned to feel quite comfortable in your newly developed skill. One skein of yarn will be enough to make three or four cloths, depending on how tightly you knit, and they can be cute and very useful gifts that can be given individually or as a set. The recipients will love the fact that these little cloths are so adorable and practical, and especially that you made them by hand. Of course, they are so adorable and practical, that you might just want to knit an extra set and keep it for yourself!

Basic Instructions

You will need:

• The 1 skein of yarn that you have chosen for The Handmade Dishcloth

• One Pair of 9" Straight Needles Size U.S. 11 / 8.0mm

• Your preferred method of counting rows

• Yarn Needles

• Scissors

If you want to use the same yarn that you used for your practice knitting, that is perfectly fine. Just make sure that it has all been ripped back from your practice fabric and that you have rewound it onto your ball of yarn. It may have a bit of a kinked appearance after you rip it back. This is no big deal and will not be noticeable once the yarn is knit into your new project.

To make The Handmade Dishcloth, pull enough yarn off your yarn ball to equal about 3 times the length of one of your knitting needles. A general rule of thumb for determining how much yarn is needed to make the cast on row for any project is to pull about 3 times the length of a row off of your yarn ball. Keep in mind that the goal is not to leave the shortest tail end of yarn possible, but instead, to leave enough of a tail end of yarn to weave in later to secure your work and to keep it from unraveling.

Start by making your slipknot at the beginning of your length of yarn. That is the side of the length that is closest to the yarn ball. Cast on 30 stitches (your slipknot counts as 1). Knit each stitch in every row for 30 rows. Yes, seriously, it is pretty much that easy. Just keep your stitches nice and relaxed, keep an accurate count of your rows, and count the stitches on your needles frequently to help keep an eye out for dropped stitches. Once you have knit your cute little square dishcloth, it is time to learn how to close up your piece.

Binding Off in Knitting

After completing any piece of knitting, you need to get your stitches off of your needle and secure them so that your piece is closed and does not unravel. This process is called "binding off" or casting off.

To bind off your dishcloth, knit the first two stitches in the usual way. Then, it's time to put your non-working needle to work! Using the tip of the non-working needle (just in case you need a gentle reminder, it's your left needle!), pick up the first stitch that you just knit and pull it up and over the second stitch, then drop it off of the needle altogether. That second stitch should still be on your non-working needle and the first stitch should now have made a little loop around the base of the second one. Just like when you made your cast on row, you want to keep your bind off row nice and loose, so take care not to over-tighten any of your bound off stitches.

Go ahead and knit another stitch. Now you will pick up the stitch closest to your right hand and pull it up and over the newest stitch. Repeat this process until you have just one stitch on your working needle.

Cut off the working yarn about 8in (20cm) away from your dishcloth. Pull the cut end of the yarn through that last stitch on your needle. This is the time to pull your yarn tight, so grab the cut end of your yarn and tighten it. This is called "fastening off" and will secure your last stitch.

You just made your first project! There is just one more step to see it through to the very end. You see those little tails of yarn hanging from your otherwise flawless work? Yeah, we're going to take care of those next.

Weaving in Your Ends

This is the final step in completing every piece of knitting you will ever do. The little tail ends of yarn left hanging from your work when you are done binding off make the piece look unfinished. You never want to tie them into knots because you would be able to feel the knots on the corners of your project. You don't want to just cut them off because eventually they will get loose and start to unravel your project. So, you have to weave the ends into the knitted piece itself and do so in a way that they will be the least visible and will be secure enough to prevent unraveling. To this end, the means will be your trusty yarn needle, so grab it and let's get to weaving in those ends.

Go ahead and thread the tail end of your yarn through the yarn needle. This is easiest by bending your yarn tightly around the needle to make a kink in the yarn and then pushing the kink through the eye of the needle.

Examine your dishcloth. Notice the pattern of raised rows and recessed rows. When weaving in your ends, you will be focusing on the raised rows. Each raised row consists of a brick-like pattern of little U's. For ease of explanation, I'm going to call each top U an umbrella and each bottom U will be called a smile. Yes, knitting is just adorable, isn't it? Each little U is going to help hide the tail end of the yarn.

Turn your dishcloth so that the tail end of yarn comes off the bottom right-hand corner. Grab your threaded yarn needle and find the smile closest to your yarn end. Insert your needle into the smile from underneath it, and then, skipping over the recessed row, insert the needle into the smile directly above the one you went through first. Gently pull your yarn through the U's. Next, you want to find the umbrella just to the left of where you came out. Follow that umbrella around, angle your needle down and to the right and insert it from the top into the smile to the left of the umbrella that you followed around. Keeping the same angle (downward and slightly to the right), insert your needle into the top of the umbrella to the bottom right of the smile. Pull your yarn through. Follow the smile directly to the left of the umbrella through which you just pulled your yarn and angling your needle up and to the right, insert your needle through the next umbrella from underneath. With the same slight angle to the right, insert your needle from underneath into the smile above and to the right of the umbrella in which your needle is inserted. Pull your yarn through. Follow the adjacent umbrella to the left, angle your needle down and to the right, and go first through the smile to the left and then through the smile below and to the right. Repeat the pattern 6 to 8 times or until your tail of yarn is too short to work through anymore stitches.

The result of weaving in the ends of yarn by using this method is a sort of figure-8 pattern. In the accompanying picture, I have woven in a contrasting color yarn so that this pattern can be clearly seen. When the ends are woven in using the same color yarn as the knitted piece, they will be virtually invisible and they will remain secure enough to prevent them from unraveling.

Once you have completed one dishcloth, go ahead and knit at least one more. This will help to ensure that the techniques you have recently learned are engrained. It will also give you more confidence as you move on to learn the next type of stitch and familiarize yourself with a couple of different knit fabrics.

Chapter 5
Your Second Project: The Easy Hat in the Round

You are really doing it! At this point in the guide, you have learned numerous new skills, quite a bit of terminology, and you have a couple of cute little finished works! You are ready to keep moving forward in your knitting adventure. So, we will cover a couple of new skills while you are knitting your next piece.

Your next project will be a beautiful and easy-to-knit hat. This is one of those projects that will really make you fall in love with your craft. It is unbelievably simple to make and looks very impressive as a finished piece.

So far, you have done all of your practice knitting and made your dishcloths on straight knitting needles. Recall that this type of knitting is called "flat knitting" because it produces flat pieces of fabric. Now, you will add a new type of knitting to your repertoire: Knitting in the Round.

34

Knitting in the round produces tubes of fabric and what is a hat, but a tube with one end closed? You are ready, so let's get started!

Basic Instructions

You will need:

- The skein of yarn that you have chosen for The Easy Hat

- One Pair of 16" Circular Needles Size U.S. 11 / 8.0mm

- Stitch Markers

- Scissors

- Yarn Needles

These instructions are to be used as a guide and to be referred back to while making your hat. Don't be alarmed if you encounter terms or techniques that have not yet been covered. You will learn them as you go.

Cast on 60 stitches. Place a stitch marker and join in the round, being careful not to twist. Knit all the stitches until the fabric measures roughly 12" (about 30cm). Decrease your rows by knitting 2 stitches together until 15 stitches remain. Break your yarn, leaving a 12" (30cm) tail. Run the tail through all the stitches on the needles. Tighten the top of the hat. Weave in all the ends.

Whew! There are several new techniques and terms in there, aren't there? Do not fret about them! We will start learning them all now. ...don't forget to wind your yarn into a ball!

Casting On in the Round

Casting on in the round is not all that different from casting on onto straight knitting needles. As you cast on in the round, hold your needle as you would hold a straight one and just let the other side sort of dangle out of your way.

Once you have all 60 stitches on your needle, place your marker. Simply slide a stitch marker onto the tip of your needle. The marker will let you know that you have reached the end of each round and after knitting the last stitch of the round, you will just slide the marker over onto your working needle. It might seem a little awkward to knit with it at first, but you will get used to it in no time.

Joining In The Round

Now that your cast on is complete, you are ready to join the ends of the row together to make a continuous, circular row called, a round.

It is interesting to note that when knitting in the round, instead of knitting row after row to make a number of neatly stacked rows as in flat knitting, you are actually knitting one long spiral row (mind blowing, isn't it?). For this reason, if an improper technique is used, there will be a little seam at the place of the join. This little seam is noticeable enough to be a minor annoyance to the knitter. And anyone who wears the hat will be constantly trying to put the seam on the side or to the back and not have it in the middle of his or her forehead. So for the sake of using the coolest tricks available to us, and for the sake of learning the best way first, we will be using what is called "an invisible join". Using this method of joining in the round completely eliminates those pesky little jogs at the join. Later on in the guide, we will cover how to avoid the jogs created when adding color.

Before joining in the round, it is crucial to make sure that the stitches on your needle are not twisted. If they are twisted around the needles when you make your join, your work will also be twisted and, thus, not viable for its intended purpose and will have to be ripped back to the beginning and started over. To make sure your stitches are not twisted, lay your needles with your cast on row flat on a surface. Examine the inside of the row. All the little knobby nubs of the cast on row should be facing the inside of the circle. If you pick it up by grabbing each end stitch on its respective needle, the cast on row will not get a chance to twist itself before we make the seamless join.

To begin the seamless join, cast on one extra stitch so that you have 61 stitches instead of the 60 stitches called for in the instructions. Pick up both needles. The working needle should be in your right hand. Knitting with the cord between your needles may be a little awkward at first. Just focus on the needle portions of the circle and let the cord fall how it will. You'll get used to it in no time. Slip the end stitch (it was the very first stitch of your cast on row) off the end of your left needle and onto your working needle. Using the tip of your left needle, scoop up the additional cast on stitch and slip that stitch over the stitch that you just slipped from your other needle and off, so that it is now forming a loop around the base of the stitch that is on the end of your working needle. Now slip the original stitch that came from the left needle back on to that left needle. You can now tighten that join down by pulling apart the tail and the working yarn. This is not one of those times that you want to take it easy and just loosely snug it. Go ahead and make it nice and tight to make the join totally disappear.

Congratulations! You have made your first seamless join in the round! You can now knit round after round until your fabric measures roughly 12" (about 31cm) in length. Remember to keep your stitches relatively relaxed and loose; to take the time to occasionally count your stitches; and to keep an eye out for dropped stitches so that they can be corrected as soon as possible. When you have reached the desired length of fabric for The Easy Hat in the Round, move on to the next section to get started on closing up the top of the hat. You're going to like this part!

Knit 2 Together

If you recall, the Basic Instructions for The Easy Hat in the Round said to "decrease the rows" by "knitting 2 stitches together". Decreasing the rows means to diminish the number of stitches in a given row, or in this case, a round. There are several techniques one can use to accomplish this, but the instructions call for doing it by means of knitting 2 stitches together. This method of decrease is by far the easiest and quickest!

It is as simple as it sounds. To decrease the rows by knitting 2 stitches together, at the beginning of the round, once you have slipped your stitch marker to your working needle, just slide the tip of your working needle into the back (from left to right, remember?) of the second stitch from the end on your left needle. Now slide the tip of the working needle through the back of the stitch on the very end of your left needle and work both stitches as if they were one. That is really all there is to it.

This is an effective means of decreasing the number of stitches because every two stitches are replaced with the one stitch that was used to work both of them simultaneously. So you are cutting the number of stitches in half with every round that you work in this way and you are getting closer and closer to finishing your adorable hat!

Finishing The Easy Hat in the Round

Follow the basic instructions for The Easy Hat in the Round and knit 2 together until there are only 15 stitches left on your needles. The instructions, at this point say to "break the yarn". If it sounds a little bit odd, it's probably because this is an out-of-date phrase for we people in the modern world who use scissors. A lot of patterns still use this phrasing, however, so it is good to know what it means.

Leave a 12" (30cm) tail on your yarn when you "break" it. Just as the basic directions say, go ahead and string that yarn tail through each of the remaining 15 stitches. For ease, you can enlist the help of your yarn needle. Just thread it with the tail of yarn and put it through all 15 stitches. Once that is done, you can safely remove your circular needles from the hat. Tighten the end of your hat by pulling on the tail of yarn until all 15 stitches come together at the center of the top of your hat. The only step that is left now is to weave in the ends!

In order to weave in the end at the top of the hat, insert your still-threaded needle down into the very center hole at the top. Now turn the hat inside out and pull the needle with the tail of yarn all the way through. Using the figure-8 technique that you learned to weave in the ends, do so with the top yarn end. When you are finished with the top yarn end, find the bottom yarn end in the rolled edge of the hat and with the hat still inside out, weave in that end using the same technique. Keep in mind that since the bottom edge of the hat rolls up, you may have to be a bit creative in effectively hiding your end to be woven in.

You just made a hat! Try it on! Give yourself a pat on the back for a job well done! You are just getting better and better at this whole knitting thing!

Chapter 6
Your Third Project: The Textured Scarf

By now you have a very good grasp of basic knitting. The concepts that, at first, seemed foreign (and maybe even a little bit intimidating) are now familiar, and the idea of making something new is exciting! You are all ready to embark on the third project in your knitting adventures: The Textured Scarf. But first, you will conquer The Purl Stitch!

The Purl Stitch

The purl stitch, like the knit stitch is a very commonly used stitch in the art of knitting. In a way that you will soon see for yourself, it is kind of the opposite of the knit stitch. The purl stitch can be used with the knit stitch to create countless fabric patterns. Patterns that have strips of texture, columns of ribbing, basket-weave type patterns, different types of lace, literally an almost endless assortment of fabric patterns can be created using the knit and purl stitches together! Learning the purl stitch will open up a whole world of knitting possibilities to you!

Grab a straight needle and your yarn, and cast on 20 stitches for your practice purl stitch swatch. Now, switch the cast on row to your left hand and pick up your working needle. Insert the tip of your working needle into your last cast on stitch from front to back (that will be from right to left, the opposite of the knit stitch).

Your working needle should be on top of your left needle (also the opposite of the knit stitch) and the two needles should form an X.

Using your left index finger to assist, slightly raise the tip of your working needle up and forward. Wrap the working yarn around the back of the working needle from the right to the left (also the opposite of the knit stitch).

With the tip of the working needle, push the yarn loop through by exiting the cast on stitch the same way it was entered. Drop the cast on stitch off of your left needle.

Closely examine your new stitch. The working yarn should now be coming off of the front of your working needle (with the knit stitch it comes off the back). Go ahead and practice 20 to 30 rows of purl stitch, stopping to count your stitches after every row and examine them frequently.

Troubleshooting

If the stitches are getting twisted, it means you are wrapping the working yarn around your needle knit-wise instead of purl-wise. If you end up with extra stitches on a row, it means that after completing your row, you need to make sure that the working yarn is coming off the front of your needle and that you are not catching it with your working needle before making your purl stitch.

Basic Instructions

You will need:

- The 2 skeins of yarn that you chose for The Textured Scarf

- One Pair of 9" Straight Needles Size U.S. 11 / 8.0mm

- A way to count rows

- Yarn needles

- Scissors

Go ahead and wind each of the skeins of yarn into their respective balls. Winding them both now will keep you from having to stop later, put down your knitting in mid-project, and wind a yarn ball. It's best if the yarn balls are ready and waiting for you.

Cast on 30 stitches. Knit the first two rows. Purl the next two rows. Continue alternating between knit and purl every two rows until you only have a 12" (30cm) tail of working yarn from your ball. It is now time to learn how to introduce a new ball of yarn in mid-project!

Once you have successfully introduced your new ball of yarn, keep knitting until your scarf is a desirable length. Then, cast off and weave in your ends.

Introducing a New Ball of Yarn

Inevitably, on some awesome project that you're working, you are going to be knitting up a storm and suddenly realize that your yarn ball has been diminished into next to nothing. Do not panic! You can easily introduce a new ball of yarn and pick up right where you left off. You won't even actually have ever left off! You will see what I mean.

When you notice that you are running low on yarn, be sure to pay close attention so that you don't get *too* low. You need to leave yourself an 8"

(20cm) – 12" (30cm) tail. It is important that you have enough of a tail from the diminishing first yarn ball that you can easily work another yarn ball into your knitting. It doesn't matter if you are smack in the middle of a row. In fact, it is best to avoid introducing a new ball of yarn at the beginning or the end of a row. This is because it can affect the tension in that edge and you want to keep that tension as consistent as possible so that your edges are nice and straight without noticeable dips and curves in them.

From the new ball of yarn, unwind a length of yarn that closely matches the tail of the yarn with which you have been working. Leaving a tail of several inches, hold the new yarn and the working yarn together. The tail of the old yarn should trail off towards the new ball. In other words, do not put the ends of the two yarns together. This can be confusing if you are thinking of the end of your original yarn ball as an actual tail. As long as it is still workable, it is your working yarn. You can imagine that the end of your old yarn still has its ball attached, if you need to, to figure out the direction in which to place the new strand of yarn. Both balls would be at the same end.

Go ahead and work both yarns together as one keeping in step with your current place in your knitting pattern. Knit both yarns together in this way for 4 or 5 stitches, keeping up your pattern, and then drop the original yarn tail. Keep knitting in your pattern with your new yarn. See that! You hardly missed a beat!

When The Patterned Scarf is a desirable length for you, you can cast off and weave in your ends. Take note that you will have to weave in two extra ends to finish your work. But, this won't be a problem for you, not at your level, you skilled knitter, you.

Chapter 7
Now You're Knitting!

You have done it! You have learned to knit and you have some fine pieces of work to prove it! Over the course of this chapter, while you bask in the glory of your accomplishments, you will learn how to change color in your flat work, how to properly change colors when knitting in the round, some basic knitting abbreviations, how to read a standard knitting pattern, and all about gauge swatches. Even though it may sound like quite a bit to digest, these practical new techniques woven in with some theoretical knowledge are going to blast you forward in your knitting adventures! We will start by getting familiar with some common stitch patterns.

A Selection of Common Stitch Patterns

It is interesting to note that when knitting, one is actually crafting fabric from a strand of yarn and using said fabric in the creation of something potentially beautiful and useful. When familiar with some common fabrics, it will be easier to lend your own creative touch to the simplest of pieces. Bear in mind, knitter, that you now possess the knowledge and the skill required to craft any and all of the following stitch patterns into their respective fabrics. You are a powerful creative force!

Garter Stitch is made by knitting each stitch in every row. It can also be made by purling each stitch in every row. It is a fabric characterized by its alternating smooth and ridged rows on both sides. Garter Stitch is a stitch pattern that is both elastic and reversible.

Stockinette Stitch is created by knitting alternating rows of knit and purl. The right side (knit side) of the fabric is smooth and is characterized by little Vs. The wrong side (purl side) is ridged. Stockinette stitch fabric has a tendency to curl up on itself at the sides and the lower edge. To make this fabric in the round, it is necessary to knit each stitch in every round.

Reverse Stockinette Stitch is also produced when alternate rows of purl and knit are used. In this fabric the right side is the purl side and the wrong side is the knit side. It is commonly used as a background for cables and other patterns that the knitter desires to stand out from the fabric.

1x1 Rib is to be worked over an even number of stitches. It is created by knitting one stitch, purling the next stitch, and repeating across a row. This fabric is very elastic and is also reversible. It is a stitch pattern characterized by the columns of smooth and bumpy stitches on both sides. It is commonly used for cuffs and neckbands on clothing because of its stretchiness.

Seed Stitch is worked over an odd number of stitches by the knit one, purl one pattern. It produces a reversible fabric that is flat and is characterized by its alternating smooth and bumpy stitches on both sides. Seed Stitch is often used as a background pattern for different motifs.

These are just a few of the near endless possibilities of stitch patterns that can be created with the two most basic of stitches in knitting: knit and purl.

Adding Stripes of Color to Your Work

This is a great tool to have in your knitting arsenal. Adding stripes of color can transform just about any work into a more interesting and aesthetically pleasing piece, and it is a very simple means of doing so.

To keep the confusion to a minimum, this technique will be explained with just 2 colors and on the assumption that the work is being knit flat. We will refer to the colors as Color 1 and Color 2, respectively.

After you have knit the desired number of rows using Color 1, pick up Color 2. Leaving a 7 or 8-inch tail, just knit your first stitch with your new color by wrapping it over the top of your working needle after you have inserted it into the first stitch of the last row. After you have knit your first stitch with Color 2, you'll notice that your new stitch is not secure and has the potential to really loosen up or even unravel if you don't deal with it. So, to tighten it up a bit, for your next 3 or 4 stitches, you will pick up both the working yarn and the tail of Color 2 and knit with both of them simultaneously. This will keep the newly added Color 2 strand of yarn nice and snug in your work with little to no chance of it working itself out of the piece. Once you are a few stitches into your row, you can drop that tail to be woven in later and just knit normally with Color 2 until the desired width of color has been obtained.

There are a few things to remember when adding stripes of color. If you plan on adding more than just a couple of rows of color at a time, you will want to cut the yarn off (leaving a tail) after knitting in your stripe each time before switching colors. Yes, this will leave many little ends for you to weave in when you finish your work, but it will also keep you from having long, unsightly floats of yarn left on the edges of your work.

Another point to take into consideration is the stitch pattern in which you are working. If you remember our Basic Stitch Patterns, you'll know that the Garter Stitch is made by knitting each stitch in every row, which makes a lovely fabric of alternating smooth and bumpy rows on both sides of the work. When an additional color is introduced into this all-knit stitch fabric, it does something kind of funky. The two sides are no longer reversible. On one side, which we can call the right side, you will have the beautiful alternating stripes of unbroken color, but on the other side, now the wrong side, the stripes will be broken up by little rows of the other color.

Some people may not mind the way it looks. It is, after all, a consistent pattern. But, it will not be the same unbroken stripes that you will get on the right side of your work. For this reason, you may decide to employ the 1x1 Rib.

The 1x1 Rib is made by simply knitting one stitch and then purling the next stitch down every row. What happens that makes the color change work so well in the 1x1 Rib is that the color changes happen in the little vertical gutters created by the purled stitches. So, the color changes are sort of tucked in and not visible unless you stretch open those purl columns. This leaves both sides of your work more uniform, thus eliminating the right side / wrong side dilemma.

I encourage you to play around with adding stripes of color to different stitch patterns to see what happens. It can be surprising how using the color changing technique in conjunction with the different patterns, can create a totally different look and you may unexpectedly stumble on a color pattern that you really love, so have fun with it!

Jog-less Color Change While Knitting in the Round

This is another wonderful skill to acquire. When you can add your own colors and do it well, you have the chance to really put some of your own personal flair into the piece that you are creating.

When knitting flat, the color can be added at the beginning of the row since the rows are stacked on top of each other in even layers of stitches. When knitting in the round, however, this is not the case. It does not produce neatly stacked rows of stitches. In fact, when knitting in the round, the knitter is actually knitting a long spiral row of stitches from start to finish (this blows my mind every time I think about it!). If a color change was to happen at the beginning of a round and if it was executed in the same way as it is when knitting flat, the result would be stripes of color with little upward jogs of stitches between colors at every point the color was changed. To avoid these little jogs, we must employ this special technique when adding color while knitting in the round.

Again, to keep confusion to minimum, we will refer to the colors as Color 1 and Color 2, and we will assume that Color 2 will be, at least 2 rounds wide. After knitting the desired length of rounds in Color 1, you are ready to switch to Color 2. At the beginning of this round, go ahead and grab Color

2. Leaving a 7 or 8-inch tail on the inside, or wrong side, of your piece, wrap the Color 2 yarn over your working needle after you have inserted it into the last stitch of the last round, just as you would for a color change while knitting flat. Work the stitch normally. Go ahead and knit the rest of the round with Color 2 and slip your stitch marker to your working needle when you get to it. Now stop for a second. Note that the stitch is loose where Color 2 was added at the start of the round and note that the little upward jog at the beginning of the first round of Color 2 can already be seen. Don't fret, knitter! We'll take care of it all soon!

To start the next round of Color 2, instead of knitting into the first stitch you worked in Color 2, you're going to find the stitch directly below it that was worked in Color 1. Insert your working needle into the right leg of that stitch from back to front so that the point of your knitting needle is now protruding through the center of the stitch between both legs. Pick up that Color 1 stitch and put it on your left needle to the right of the Color 2 stitch. Knit the Color 1 stitch and the Color 2 stitch together as if they were one stitch. Continue on knitting your round.

When you get to the end of the second round in Color 2, pause and take notice that the color change illusion is quite convincing! There is no visible telltale upward jog on the right side of your work. It appears that miraculously, the color change was made as if each round were actually stacked on top of one another as is the way when knitting flat! Ah, but wait! What about that loose stitch at the very beginning of the color change? It's time to deal with that now.

It is highly recommended that you do not wait too long to weave in the ends of these color changes. They are loose and can affect the stitches around them, too. So, after no more than a few rounds in Color 2, grab your yarn needle and prepare to do some weaving!

Thread your yarn needle with the Color 2 tail of yarn that you left at the beginning of the color change round. Using your figure 8 weaving technique that you learned in the Weaving in Your Ends section of this guide, weave the end into the inside, or wrong side, of the work. This will secure that first stitch that you made in Color 2 and the stitches around it will once again be safe.

These techniques should be used for every color change while knitting in the round. So when you are ready to switch back to Color 1, you will do it in the same way as you just did with Color 2. Leaving a tail, add in the new color. Knit a round. At the start of the second round, knit into both the first stitch of round 1 and the stitch below it by grabbing the stitch below form the back of its right leg and placing it on your left needle next to the first stitch of the round. Knit another row. Weave in your ends.

You can now add jog-less stripes of color to your works while knitting in the round! You will enjoy personalizing your round works with color stripes and you won't have to worry about the little upward jogs, because you know what you're doing!

Basic Knitting Abbreviations

The vast majority of knitting patterns that you encounter in your knitting adventures will have abbreviations that are standard to the written language of knitting. Some patterns include an abbreviation key, while others just expect you to know what they mean. A knitting-shorthand of sorts, these abbreviations make it easier to write patterns as well as to read them. It is here that you will find a chart defining some of the most common knitting abbreviations and their meanings. Once you are familiar with most of them, reading standard knitting patterns will be a breeze.

Abbr	Description
[ ]	work instructions within brackets as many times as indicated
( )	work instructions within parentheses in the place indicated
*	repeat instructions following asterisk as indicated
approx	approximately
Beg	beginning
Bet	between
BO	bind off
Cn	cable needle
CO	cast on
Cont	continue
Dec	decrease
Inc	increase
K	Knit
K2tog	knit two together

lp(s)	loop(s)
M1	make one stitch
P	Purl
pat(s)	pattern(s)
Pm	place marker
P2tog	purl two together
Prev	previous
Rem	remain/remaining
Rep	repeat(s)
rev St st	reverse stockinette stitch
rnd(s)	round(s)
RS	right side
sk	Skip
sl	Slip
sl st	slip stitches
st(s)	stitch(es)
St st	stockinette stitch
tog	together
WS	wrong side
wyib	with yarn in back
wyif	with yarn in front
YO	yarn over

Reading a Written Knitting Pattern

Up to now, the "Basic Instructions" you have received for each of your projects have served as a sort of an introduction to reading knitting patterns. The time has now come for you to learn how to read an actual standard knitting pattern. These patterns are not all that difficult to decipher, but they do require a certain level of understanding as far as terminology, abbreviations, and techniques are concerned. You can definitely be confident about it, since at this point in the adventure, you are fully capable and you already possess that understanding.

Written knitting patterns can, of course, vary greatly in complexity, depending on the difficulty of the work for which the pattern is written, but generally, they all share a few basic components.

Somewhere in the beginning of the pattern, there will be a section devoted to the materials that are required to complete the piece. This might be written as "Materials Required" or "What You'll Need" or even something different. But, this section will list the type and size of knitting needles; the type, weight, and amount of yarn; and any other equipment required to complete the project.

Many of the more complex patterns will tell you to make a gauge swatch, especially if the item being knit is to be a specific size like many articles of clothing. Gauge refers to how many stitches and rows of stitches that there are in a given measured area. A swatch is a test piece of knitting made to determine if the numbers of stitches and rows that you knit are comparable to the numbers of stitches and rows required to make an item to match the measurements of a specific size. Gauge swatches are covered in depth later in this chapter. For now, you need to know that sometimes they are included in proper written knitting instructions.

Some written knitting patterns will, at this point, have a separate section for cast on instructions. Other patterns will include the cast on instructions in the section about actually knitting the given piece. Either way, you will know how many stitches to cast on and anything else you might need to know about that cast on row.

There will be a section with "Row, Stitch" information. This section is kind of the meat of your pattern in that these are the directions that you will follow in order to actually craft the piece. If there are different instructions for each row, you will see that. If there are different instructions for every few stitches, you will see that. This section will also let you know when and how you are to bind off your work. The "Row, Stitch" section will almost always be written using abbreviations in place of common knitting terms.

Some patterns will include a section that interprets and explains the abbreviations that were used in the "Row, Stitch" section. This can be extremely helpful, especially for the beginner to intermediate level knitters, who still might be familiarizing themselves with many of the common terms and abbreviations used in knitting. Unfortunately, not all written knitting patterns include this section. Do not fear, though! You can always refer back to the section of this guide with the handy table of common knitting abbreviations, and it will help you decipher a lot of those seemingly mysteriously coded knitting abbreviations!

Since, you already have several projects under your knitting belt, we will look at a proper written knitting pattern of a couple of those projects. It will be easier for you to read having already followed the instructions and having actually crafted the piece. We will start by taking a look at The Handmade Dishcloth in its written pattern form.

The Handmade Dishcloth

Materials Required:

• One skein of medium-weight yarn, a 3 or a 4

• One Pair of 9" Straight Needles Size U.S. 11 / 8.0mm

• A row counter

• Yarn needles

Cast on 30 sts.
K all sts for 30 rows.
BO
Weave in ends.

There you have it: your first project's written pattern! It's short, concise, and very straight to the point. Now, let's take a look at one of your more complex completed projects in written knitting pattern form, The Easy Hat in the Round.

The Easy Hat in the Round.

Materials Required:

• One skein medium weight yarn, 3 or 4

• One Pair of 16" Circular Needles Size U.S. 11 / 8.0mm

• Stitch Marker

• Yarn Needles

CO 60 sts.

K all sts for 12".
K2tog to dec sts until 15 sts rem.
Leaving a 12" tail, break yarn.
Run tail through all rem sts. and down into center of closure at top of hat.
Weave in ends on WS of hat.

Again, the written knitting pattern is short, concise, and straight to the point. It's really a beautiful thing, isn't it?

Now, eventually, somewhere along the line in your knitting adventures, you will read a written knitting pattern and inevitably you will encounter an abbreviation with which you are not familiar. It is perfectly acceptable to employ your favorite search engine to assist you in breaking the secret code of the unknown abbreviation.

Gauge Swatches: What Are They and How To Make Them

So far, in our guide, you have not been required to make any gauge swatches. They have not been necessary to craft any of the projects you have completed. There will come a day in your knitting adventures, however that you are knitting a clothing article that has a specific size, or a bag that needs to be the correct length to work with its closure, or the like. When your knitted piece needs to be as close as possible to the given measurements in a pattern, you will need to make a gauge swatch to facilitate this.

Gauge refers to the number of stitches and rows in a given area of knitting. A swatch is a small piece of knitting made and used to achieve the same gauge that was used in a given knitting pattern's instructions. Obtaining a gauge that is accurate ensures that the knitter will achieve the proper measurements given in said pattern. Thus, the gauge swatch is employed.

In order to make an accurate gauge swatch, it is usually recommended that you knit a 4" (10cm) by 4" (10cm) swatch. Some patterns will only require you to know your gauge in 1" (2.5cm) by 1" (2.5cm), but most written knitting patterns that mention a gauge swatch at all, will want you to use the 4" by 4" swatch. Be sure to use the specific yarn and specific size needles suggested by the pattern to create your swatch. Unless otherwise specified, by your pattern, you will knit your gauge swatch in Stockinette Stitch. That's the stitch pattern that is made by knitting alternating rows of knit and pearl. It produces little V's that will be easy to count.

After creating your gauge swatch, you will want to wash and block it. This will also improve the accuracy of the swatch. Since many yarns and fabrics behave differently once they have been washed and blocked, it would be counterproductive and frustrating to go through the trouble of making your gauge swatch and measuring it to compare to your pattern, then knitting your piece only to find out that when your piece is washed and blocked it is no longer in the same gauge as was your swatch! If blocking is an unfamiliar term to you, there's no need to worry; blocking knitted pieces is covered in Chapter 10 of this guide.

Lay your swatch flat. If it is curling at the ends, you may want to pin it down to an ironing board or something similar to keep it flat. If you have to pin it, take care not to stretch it out, this will affect the accuracy of your measurement. Using a measuring tape or a ruler, measure out four inches horizontally on your swatch along the length of a row. Now, while pressing the measuring device flat against your swatch with your fingers, use a yarn needle or knitting needle (something with a point will make it easier to see while you are counting) in your free hand. With the tip of your needle, follow along the edge of the measuring device, counting each stitch in the row just above it. When you have that number, make a note of it and compare it to the gauge required by the pattern that you are trying to match. If it matches up, you are good to go!

If your gauge does not match up with that given by your pattern, there are a few things that you can try to get it as close as possible. It is important to note that if your gauge swatch is different than the one in the pattern, it is not because you have done anything wrong! The tension with which we knitters knit can vary pretty impressively from person to person. One person might consistently knit very loosely, while another person consistently uses more tension and produces knitting that is considerably tighter. This is part of the reason why it is a good idea to make gauge swatches. So, don't be discouraged! Just try the following fixes!

If your gauge has fewer stitches than are called for in your pattern, you can aim to knit a little bit tighter or try using the next needle size down from the one suggested by the pattern. Conversely, if you have more stitches in your gauge than what is called for, try knitting a bit more loosely or try using the next needle size up from the one suggested by the pattern.

Gauge swatches may seem like a knitting step one could avoid, especially if you are anxious to get to the good part: the actual knitting of your project. But, these swatches really are a time and effort-saving tool when you need to make something that matches the measurements given in your knitting pattern. So, if your piece is to be a specific size, make sure your gauge swatch measures up!

Chapter 8
Blocking Your Work

Not all knitted items are perfect as soon as you bind that last stitch off. They can have waves in the fabric that cause them to look lumpy and bumpy; they can have edges that are supposed to lie flat, but refuse to do so; they can pull together towards the middle making them have a shrunken appearance; or they can be overly relaxed and lose their intended shape. Yes, sometimes your knitted works will behave like unruly children. The remedy in this case is not harsh punishment. Those defiant stitches just need to be lovingly and thoughtfully told how you expect them to behave and they need to be put into a sort of knitting time-out with care where they can gently learn their lesson. So we will tame our unruly pieces of knitting by blocking them!

Silly metaphors aside, blocking is not only a means of taming disagreeable pieces of work, but it is also a great way to get some of the more delicate patterns to stand out and be seen. Laces, eyelets, and similar finely detailed work will benefit from being blocked. The patterns in the fabric will be much more obvious, and therefore the beautiful details of your work will be much more appreciated.

There are three basic types of blocking. Each type of blocking involves a different method of dampening the knitted work. Then, the work is shaped and left to dry. When choosing which type of blocking is appropriate for a given fiber, it is best to refer to the care instructions on the ball band of the yarn. If no care instructions are available, you can always test a method of blocking on a gauge swatch to see what works for the fiber of your piece. Sounds simple enough, right? It really is.

You will need:

• A blocking board

Fancy blocking boards designed specifically for blocking fabrics are available, but many knitters use the interlocking children's foam play squares since they are inexpensive, can be reused over and over, and can be added on to in order to block larger items. If you are blocking a small item, an ironing board might even work. Just make sure that your blocking board surface is slightly larger that your knitted piece to block.

- T-pins

These are sharp pins with a horizontal bar at the top that makes a T. They can easily be found at any craft store and online. Make sure the T-pins you purchase are rust-free. If you are planning to use the steam blocking method, take note that you do not want to buy the T-pins with the cute little colored plastic coating on their horizontal bars. When hit with hot steam from an iron, that plastic coating has the potential to melt and if it did, it would ruin your beloved knitted work.

- Towels

Use a couple of clean towels to protect your work surface from water. They will also help evenly distribute the water. Note that depending on the yarn material with which you knitted and the dyes used to color it, the colors from your yarn could potentially run and get on your towels, so for this reason, it's a good idea not to use your best white towels.

Wet Blocking

Wet blocking is acceptable for the following materials: angora, cotton, linen, mohair, wool, wool blends, and wool-like fibers such as cashmere and alpaca. For synthetic fabrics, it is best to refer to the care instructions on the ball band.

For wet blocking, in addition to the supplies listed above, you will also need:

- A wash or soak

There are all kinds of recommendations for what wash or soak one should use when wet blocking. Some knitters like to use baby shampoo, while others prefer a wool-wash detergent, some will even recommend using mild dish soap. All of these choices will involve rinsing your piece thoroughly. There are also some non-rinse formulated soaks available that eliminate the rinse step. Keep in mind, that if you choose a wash or soak that is scented your knitting is going to bear the same scent.

- A basin large enough to hold your work and the water in which you will wash or soak it

- A few extra towels to press some of the water out of your work before pinning.

Begin by either diluting your soak according to its directions or by diluting your chosen wash to roughly 2 tsp / 1 gallon of water in the basin. Remember that you will have to rinse out whatever kind of wash you use, so be conservative when adding it to the water. Place the knitted piece to be blocked into the solution and gently turn it over with your hands, agitating it just enough to wet thoroughly and to distribute the solution throughout the knitted piece. Be gentle! Remove the knitted work from the solution after it has been saturated and rinse it well, that is, unless you are using a non-rinse soak. Again, gentleness is a must! Carefully lay your piece between a couple of towels and press out the excess water. You never, ever want to wring out a knitted piece as it will overstretch and misshape the stitches, which is pretty much opposite to the goal of blocking your work. Keep pressing out the excess water until your piece is no longer drenched, but just damp.

After, the excess water has been removed, cover your backing board with a dry towel or towels. Some knitters choose to place a garbage bag between their blocking board and the towel layer in order to expedite the drying process. Carefully, lay your piece of knitting out on the towel or towels, shaping it as much as possible by hand before pinning. Grab your T-pins and pin down the corners of the piece first, followed by the midpoints. Be generous on the number of pins you use to evenly distribute any tension along the edges of the work. If you use too few pins, your piece will end up with noticeable points along the edges where the pins were. Remember, that you can use blocking to stretch out any areas where you may have knitted more tightly than others in order to give the stitches a more uniform appearance. Additionally, you want to pin at the feature areas in order to showcase any fine detail work like open stitched rows and along fine edging.

Allow your piece to dry completely before removing the pins. This may take a few hours or a couple of days, depending on how damp the piece is when it is blocked, the weight of the yarn used, and the thickness of the stitch pattern. For instance, a delicate lace knit from a light yarn is obviously going to be dry before a piece with thick cables that was knit with a bulky yarn.

Spray or Spritz Blocking

Spray, or spritz blocking, as it's sometimes called is acceptable for blocking the following materials: angora, mohair, wool, wool blends, and wool-like fibers like alpaca and cashmere. Again, refer to the care instructions on the ball band of the yarn used, before wetting down any piece made from a synthetic fiber yarn.

Spray blocking is different from wet blocking in the sense that instead of submersing your knitted piece and using wash or soak, you simply spray it down with water from a spray bottle to dampen it. This method is great for flat pieces as well as pieces that will be blocked on a form.

Forms are helpful in blocking knit pieces that cannot really be laid flat like hats or cowls. There are, of course, a wide range of inexpensive to expensive forms available that are designed specifically for these types of purposes, but if you can find something close to the size and shape you need, like a bowl or a vase turned upside down, then that should suffice.

To spray block on a form, simply spray the work until damp, then place it onto the form, shape it, and allow it to dry. To spray block flat on a blocking board, just spray the work until damp instead of soaking or washing and then rinsing, as in wet blocking, and then follow the same directions for shaping and pinning the piece to the blocking board.

Steam Blocking

Steam blocking is suitable for blocking pieces that have been knit from the following materials: cotton, linen, wool and wool-like fibers such as cashmere and alpaca. Silk can be steam blocked, but the delicacy of the silk fibers can make it risky. Caution must, also, be taken when steam blocking knit work made from acrylic or acrylic blends. If the acrylic gets too hot, its fibers can melt together, so that when they cool they actually harden, thus, ruining your work. So, if you have a wool blend or cotton blend, you should definitely check the ball band on the yarn for care instructions before applying steam. Though, wool and cotton are natural fibers and can stand up to the heat, whatever other fibers may have been blended with them, may not be so tough.

For steam blocking, you will need an iron with steam capability or a hand-held steamer and an ironing board or a thick layer of towels on your backing board. There is no need to dampen the work before steam blocking. You can just get right to it. Adjust the settings on your iron or steamer to produce the maximum amount of steam. While holding the iron or the steamer just above the piece, with the other hand, very carefully shape the fabric of the piece as you go. Be very careful! That steam is very hot, of course! Also, remember never to set the steaming iron or steamer directly on the piece. You want to keep the device hovering just above it and keep it moving. Don't let it hover too long over one spot.

When you have gone over one side of the piece of knitting, turn it over and steam the other side. If your knitted piece is a stitch pattern of lace or eyelet, you will want to stretch open the pattern as you steam the work. Repeat this process as many times as necessary to achieve the desired look.

Steam blocking is sometimes favored over other blocking techniques since it is much faster. The need for soaking or washing and the subsequent drying time is not a factor, so you are freed up sooner to get right back to knitting your next piece of art!

Chapter 9
Your Fourth Project: The Cabled Headband

Many people, when they think of knitting, think of the quintessential hand crafted sweater with the big cables knitted into it. It seems that somehow those cables became associated with knitting by hand and that is the image that a lot of folks draw to when knitting is brought up as a subject matter. Maybe this rings true for you and maybe not. Either way, cables are undisputedly, a beautiful way to add interesting detail to many a knitted work. They are very rewarding to make, as well, since they look like a lot more work than they actually are, which is always a bonus for the craftsperson!

For your introduction to knitting cables, an entire sweater seems like a bit of overkill, so we will start small. We'll begin with a very manageable project called, The Cabled Headband. This is one of those kinds of projects that does not take very much time to finish and that you can use 1 skein of yarn to make several pieces. These little headbands make great gifts, by the way!

Since you are now adept at reading written knitting patterns, the instructions will be presented in that form. This will help you to become even more comfortable seeing them and working from them before you spread your crafty wings and fly out on your own into the bigger world of knitting.

Notice in the "Materials Required" section that you will need to make another craft store run or put in another online order for a few more supplies before you get started. So grab your supplies and prepare yourself! This is going to be a lot of fun!

The Pattern

The Cabled Headband

Materials Required:

•1 skein of worsted weight yarn

• U.S. size 4 (3.5mm) needles

- A cable needle

Abbreviations:

K (knit), P (purl), sl st (slip stitch)

Instructions:

This pattern is to be worked over 8 rows.
Cast on 16 sts.
Rows 1, 3, 5, 7: K4, P8, K4.
Rows 2, 4, 6: K16
Row 8: K4, sl 4 sts onto cn, and hold to back, K4, then K the 4 sts from the cn, K4

Rep these 8 rows 19 times.
Rep row 1.
BO
Break yarn, leaving an 8" (20cm) to 12" (30.5cm) tail.
Join edges together.
Steam block if necessary.

You probably noticed a few new abbreviations and a couple of unfamiliar instructions in the Cabled Headband pattern. For the abbreviations, if you have not already referred to the Basic Knitting Abbreviations section of this guide, please, do so now. For the unfamiliar instructions, sit back and relax! We will cover those as we go!

Take note that this pattern requires the knitter to count rows, but does not include a row counter in the "Materials Required" section. It assumes that you have a way to count rows. It also directs you to "Join edges together". That requires a yarn needle, which again, the pattern assumes that you have. Some patterns are just going to be like that.

The new piece of equipment introduced in this pattern is a cable needle (cn). Cable needles are available wherever knitting needles are sold. They are generally pretty thin and only about 4" (10cm) to 5" (12.5cm) long. They are pointed on both ends, but are not sharp, and they have a jog in the center. The interesting thing about cable needles is that they are not absolutely necessary to knit cables. Other tools can be used to accomplish the same job that a cable needle accomplishes. This is rather odd, I know. The shape of the cable needle really does make knitting cables a bit easier, though. So, it is advisable to use one.

Notice at the very beginning of the "Knit, Row" section of the pattern, it says, "This pattern is to be worked over 8 rows." That simply means that it takes 8 rows of knitting from the instructions to complete one cycle of this pattern. The cycle is to be repeated 19 times for this particular pattern. Remember The Patterned Scarf? The instructions were to k 2 rows, p 2 rows. So that pattern is worked over 4 rows. After the 4th row, the pattern is to be repeated. Most written knitting patterns that include detail work or any kind of pattern in the rows will say, "This pattern is to be worked over (so many) rows." It's a very common phrase in knitting language.

Making Cables

Again, cables are an absolutely beautiful way to decorate the fabric of certain works. They do not work in every piece, but when they do work, they bring the level of detail to a whole new level. The Cabled Headband is a relatively simple project and a great one to get you knitting with cables. Once you know how to work a simple cable, crafting the more intricate and complex cables are no longer out of reach to you. Learning to knit cables is another one of those skills that will allow you to really propel yourself forward toward the mastery of your craft.

Up to row 8 in the pattern for The Cabled Headband, you should be knitting like pro! When you get to Row 8, knit your 4 stitches and then slip the next four stitches on to the cable needle. The instructions require that you "hold to back," so carefully put the cable needle holding the four stitches behind (on the other side from you) your knitting needle points. Go ahead and knit the next 4 stitches to the right of the stitches on the cable needle. Then pull the cable needle and its 4 stitches back to the front of the points of the knitting needle and slip them back on to your left needle. Knit them normally. It might take some getting used to because the yarn will pull a bit since it will be stretched over the other stitches, but you will grow accustomed to it quickly. After you have knit the stitches from the cable needle, continue knitting the remaining 4 stitches on the row.

You have just successfully knit your first cable! Congratulations! Just keep repeating the 8 row pattern until you have done it 19 more times and you will be all set to bind off and join your edges together.

Joining Edges Together

Sometimes, as in the case of The Cabled Headband, it is necessary to join edges of knitted pieces together. Joining the edges, or seaming as it's sometimes called, of multiple pieces can also be used to make very large works from a number of smaller ones, as well as piecing together oddly shaped pieces that would be very difficult to knit as a whole piece. For The Cabled Headband, you just need to join two straight and relatively short edges, so it is a perfect project to familiarize yourself with this technique.

To begin, set the headband out flat and bring together the edges to be joined so that the long tail from your bind off row is on the right and you are looking at the right side of your work. You will use that tail to seam the edges together. Thread your yarn needle using the tail from the bind off row.

It is very important that the stitches from the cast on row match up exactly to the stitches from the bind off row. It is advisable that you count the stitches as you go so that the first stitch of the cast on row matches up with the first stitch of the bind off row, and the second stitches of both rows match up, and the third stitches, etc.

From right to left, place the tip of the needle into the stitch directly to the left of the first cast on stitch. Pull the needle and yarn through. Take care not to over-tighten it. This will cause it to bunch up and leave a scar-like seam as opposed to a relaxed joined edge. From left to right, place the tip of your yarn needle into the stitch directly to the right of the second bind off stitch. Pull the needle and yarn through. Repeat this matching up the stitches until all the stitches have been seamed. Turn the headband inside out and weave in the ends on the wrong side of your work. You now have your first cabled piece! Didn't I tell you it was going to be fun?

Chapter 10
Your Fifth Project: A Dishcloth on the Bias

Ok, Knitter Extraordinaire! Having first-hand knitting knowledge of many, many techniques now and having crafted numerous beautiful and functional pieces, at this point you are moving right along in your knitting adventures!

While making this cute little dishcloth you are going to quickly and easily learn two knitting techniques that are very commonly called for in a multitude of written knitting patterns: knitting on the bias and the yarn over. Let's get started!

The Pattern

A Dishcloth on the Bias

Materials Required:

• A medium weight yarn, a 4

• U.S. size 7 (4.5mm) knitting needles

Instructions:

CO 4 sts.
Row 1: K4
Row 2: K2, YO, K all rem sts in row
Rep Row 2 until you have 44 sts on the needle
Row 3: K1, K2tog, YO, k2tog, K all rem sts in row
Rep Row 3 until you have 4 sts on the needle
BO

Seems easy enough, right? That's because it will be!

Knitting on the Bias

Knitting on the bias is another very easy way to add a little more of a design element to a piece. As you can probably tell from the written pattern for these dishcloths, it is not difficult. Basically, you just start out knitting from a corner of your work and increase stitches to the middle of the piece. Once the midline is reached, the remaining rows are knit while decreasing the number of stitches back down to the number of stitches with which you began. Instead of producing neatly stacked little horizontal rows, knitting in this way produces neatly stacked little diagonal rows. The diagonal rows create an element of visual interest that is both very easy to make, and very pleasing to the eye.

Yarn Over

If you think back to The Easy Hat in the Round, when it was time to bring the hat to its point and closing it up, you decreased the number of stitches on your needle by repeatedly knitting 2 of them together. The yarn over is used to do the opposite. Each yarn over will actually create an additional stitch, which is also called an increase. In addition to increasing the number of stitches on your needle, each yarn over, coincidentally, also leaves a little hole, or window, in your work. These little windows may look like mistakes at first, but they can be used to give a piece a little extra something to make it more visually interesting. What's more exciting is that the yarn over is a very common technique used to make lace patterns! Once you master this simple technique, you will be able to confidently tackle projects that produce beautiful and sometimes intricate lace designs. And, much like most of the techniques you have already learned, it is much easier than it looks!

So, follow your written knitting pattern until you get to the instructions for Row 2. Now, just like the pattern calls for you to do, knit 2 stitches. For your yarn over, simply bring the working yarn around and over your working needle from right to left. So you will wrap the yarn around the back of the working needle and bring it to the front. Then, as the pattern instructs, finish knitting across the remainder of that row.

Pause here and examine the place in your work where you performed the yarn over. Gently stretch the area out with your fingers so that you can get a good look at what the yarn over looks like. You should be able to see a strand of yarn on your needle between two stitches and just below the strand of yarn should be your little window created by the yarn over. Isn't that adorable...and oh so easy!

Go ahead and finish knitting according to the written pattern instructions. When you are finished, take a moment to appreciate your work! You will be the proud creator and owner of a cute little dishcloth, which you have knit on the bias!

Chapter 11
A Collection of Projects to Keep You Going

You are knitting up a storm now! You have so many tools in your knitting arsenal that you are ready to really let your creativity soar. Because you are so ready, this chapter will be more about allowing you to use the skills you have acquired throughout your journey so far, and less about receiving detailed instruction on new techniques. You will definitely still learn a thing or two, but since the detailed instruction on every little thing is not required anymore, you will be learning those things considerably more independently. You will, again, amaze yourself at how quickly you will pick things up, now that you have come so far! Happy Knitting!

Yarn Over Shawl With Drop Stitch Detail

You are going to love this project! This pattern is for a gorgeous shawl that will get you very comfortable with the yarn over. We will also introduce a brand new skill: the drop stitch.

Up until now, a dropped stitch has been considered to be the enemy of smooth, trouble-free knitting. It has been viewed as an annoyance, as a problem that needed correcting as soon as possible. Well, now we are going to harness the power of the dropped stitch and use it for good, instead of evil.

If you remember back to the section about correcting dropped stitches, you will recall that when a stitch is dropped, as it runs, it leaves little un-worked horizontal bars in its wake. Those little horizontal bars, as ugly as they can be when you are not expecting them, can be quite a nifty design element when they are used to a knitter's advantage. And that is just what we are going to do with them.

The Pattern:

Materials Required:

• Roughly 200 to 210 yards / 40g of a medium weight yarn in a wool blend

• U.S. Size 10 (6mm) knitting needles

Instructions:

Loosely CO 30 sts.
Row 1: * K2, YO *, Rep across row, end in K2.
* K a row, P a row * for a total of 128 rows, ending on a WS row.
Next row (RS): * K2, drop stitch *, Rep across row, end in K2.
BO loosely.
Block the piece as long and as wide as you can possibly stretch it.

When you get to the "drop stitch row", after knitting 2 stitches as is directed, you will simply slide the next stitch off of your left needle without working it. It may seem counterintuitive at this point to just purposely drop a stitch off the needle, but you will be very pleased with the results!

Keep in mind that you want to encourage the dropped stitches to run. To do this, just gently stretch them. The more the dropped stitches are stretched, the more they will open up. And it is by opening up, that this visually interesting detail will be more noticeable.

Elongated Stitch Scarf

This gorgeous and very easy scarf is sure to become one of your favorite pieces to knit. It makes for a beautiful gift and like a lot of your completed knitting projects, it looks very fancy and detailed, but doesn't require nearly as much work as one might think, so you can definitely take time to knit one for yourself, too!

If you recall your last project, The Yarn Over Shawl With Drop Stitch Detail, you were instructed to drop stitches in order to create their telltale horizontal bars and use them as visual and textural detail. Well, the elongated stitch is a close relative of the drop stitch. In fact, they are often confused. To clarify, the drop stitch is used to produce horizontal strands and the dropping of the stitch takes place after knitting where the column of horizontal stitches is to be. The elongated stitch produces vertical strands and is performed on the row that is knit following a row where there was a yarn over. The elongated stitch is, basically, a combination of the yarn over and the drop stitch. You will see exactly what I mean when you get to knitting.

The Pattern:

Materials Required:

- 1 skein worsted weight yarn

- Knitting needles of appropriate size for the yarn (see yarn ball band)

The Pattern:

CO 26 sts
K 4 rows.
Start pattern:
Row 1: K6, * YO, K1, 2YO, K1, 3YO, K1, 2YO, K1, YO, K6 *
Rep bet ** all the way across. (You will do the rep 2ce)
Row 2: K across, dropping all the YO's as you go
Row 3: K across
Row 4: K across
Row 5: K1, * YO, K1, 2YO, K1, 3YO, K1, 2YO, K1, YO, K6 *
Rep bet ** across the row. (You will do the rep 3 times on this row) On the last rep, end with K1 instead of K6.
Row 6: K across, dropping all YO's as you go
Row 7: K across
Row 8: K across
Continue the pattern until you run low on yarn or until the scarf reaches the desired length.
End with K 4 rows.
Weave in ends.
Wash and block the finished piece to open up the pattern.

You will be dropping the yarn overs in this project to make the elongated stitches. When you get to a row that requires this action, simply slip the yarn overs off of your left needle as you go. There will be knit stitches on the same rows as the yarn overs. Don't worry about getting them confused and dropping the wrong stitches. By now, you will be able to tell the difference at a glance. Remember, the yarn overs have not been worked as the stitches have. They have no loop around their bases and they will have their little windows directly underneath them. You will undoubtedly know them when you see them.

Finish the scarf according to the written pattern and be prepared, once again, to be impressed with your own abilities! This project produces an absolutely stunning piece of work!

Double Pattern Cowl

The bulkier and softer the yarn is for this 2-pattern cowl, the better! Easily knit in the round, this piece would look great in a bright, solid color yarn to bring out the differences in the stitch patterns. This is a very quick-to-knit project with extremely satisfying results.

The Pattern:

Materials Required:

- 100 yards of super-bulky yarn

- 16" (40.5cm) U.S. size 15 (10mm) circular knitting needles

Instructions:

Loosely CO 48 sts.
Being careful not to twist, perform the seamless join.
Work * K2, P2 * rib for 14 rows.
After the first 14 rows in the rib are complete, start the 2nd stitch pattern.
This pattern is to be worked over 4 rows.
Row 1: * K1, P1 * around
Row 2: * K1, P1 * around
Row 3: * P1, K1 * around
Row 4: * P1, K1 * around
Rep first 4 rows to make a total of 16 rows.
BO loosely.
Weave in ends.

Was that not the quickest project ever? And, I know it looks amazing! Good for you, fellow knitter!

Quick Leg Warmers

This is another very quick and easy project to knit in the round. These leg warmers would look great with an improvised cable or even knit with a variegated yarn. They are so simple and cleanly designed, that the option for your creativity to leave its mark on these cute little pieces is wide open.

So, maybe knit a plain pair and then after you see how quick and easy they really are, you can play with the design by experimenting with different texture and color combinations.

The Pattern:

Materials Required:

- Approx 400 yards of worsted weight yarn

- 16" (41cm) U.S. size 4 (3.5mm) circular knitting needles

- 16" (41cm) U.S. size 7 (4.5mm) circular knitting needles

Instructions:

With the smaller needles, CO 64 sts.
PM
Taking care not to twist, perform an invisible join.
Work all sts in 2x2 Rib (K2, P2) for 2.5in (6cm)
Switch to larger needles and K all sts in every rnd until the work measures 10.5in (26cm).
Switch back to smaller needles and work in 2x2 rib for another 2.5in (6cm).
BO loosely.
Weave in ends.
Make your second leg warmer!

A note about switching knitting needle sizes when in mid-piece: do not try to slip all the stitches off of one size needle and on to the next. There is no need to go to that kind of trouble. Simply, start the next round by using your new sized knitting needle as your working needle. Work the stitches in that round as directed by the pattern, and when you are done with the round, see that all of your stitches have been transferred to your desired sized needles. It's easy!

Luxury Cowl

This cowl is so quick and so easy, but it looks so luxurious and expensive, you are bound to keep using this pattern over and over. Both the fluted texture and its appearance that result from this pattern are absolutely beautiful. A seamless piece, knit it in the round, it is best when made with a bulky, soft yarn.

The Pattern:

Materials Required:

- 4 skeins of medium to bulky weight yarn

- 16" U.S. size 9 (5.5mm) circular knitting needles

Instructions:

To be worked over 8 rows.
CO 82 sts.
Pm for beg of rnd.
Taking care not to twist sts, perform an invisible join.
Rnds 1-4: P all sts
Rnds 5-8: K all sts
Rep rnds 1-8 until cowl measures 21" (54cm).
End with a rnd 4.
BO
Weave in ends.

The big bulky yarn is fun and easy to knit, and will produce quite a large piece. It is big enough to wear not only as a cowl, but can be pulled up in the back and over the back of the head to be worn as a lush hood for a very chic look!

Eyelet Scarf

The Eyelet Scarf will make great use of your skills to increase and decrease stitches using the yarn over and the knit 2 together techniques, respectively. And the little windows, or eyelets, created by the yarn overs give this scarf a delicate, lacy touch. It is a lovely piece to add to your personal collection or to make for a loved one.

The Pattern:

Materials Required:

- 2 skeins of medium to bulky weight yarn

- U.S. size 11 (8mm) knitting needles

Instructions:

CO 20 sts.
Row 1: K across
Row 2: K across
Row 3: K across
Row 4: K across
Row 5: K2, * YO, K2tog*
Rep bet ** to last 2 sts of row, K2.
Rep rows 1-5 until desired length is reached, ending on Row 4.
BO
Break yarn.
Weave in ends.
Block to open up the eyelet pattern.

Cable Scarf

If you love the look and feel of cables, this scarf is a must-knit! The beautiful cable pattern that runs the length of the piece, gives the scarf weight and warmth. An absolutely gorgeous piece, this one will take some time, but the finished result is well worth it: a beautiful and functional scarf that you will be very proud to have made.

The Pattern:

Materials Required:

- Approx 350 yards of worsted weight yarn
- U.S. size 8 (5mm) knitting needles

- Cable needle

Instructions:

CO 42 sts
Row 1: (WS) K2, P2, K2, P6, K2, P2, K2, P6, K2, P2, K2, P6, K2, P2, K2
Row 2: (RS) K4, P2, K6, P2, K2, P2, K6, P2, K2, P2, K6, P2, K4

Row 3: (WS) Rep row 1.
Row 4: (RS) Rep row 2.
Row 5: (WS) Rep row 1.
Row 6: (RS) Rep row 2.
Row 7: (WS) Rep row 1.
Row 8: (RS) K4, P2, C6F, P2, K2, P2, C6F, P2, K2, P2, C6F, P2, K4
Rep the 8 rows until scarf is the desired length, ending on Row 7.
BO

In The Cabled Headband pattern, you were instructed to slip the stitches to be cabled onto the cable needle and hold them to the back of your work. Notice that the pattern for the Cable Scarf instructs you to "C6F". That means that you will slip 3 (yes 3!) stitches onto your cable needle and hold them to the front of your work, then you will knit the next 3 stitches, and to finish the same instruction, you will knit the stitches off the cable needle. All that information was to be gleaned from "C6F".

It is very important to keep in mind that not all cabled pieces are made in exactly the same way and not all written patterns for cable designs will read exactly the same. There are numerous ways to make cables. Any number of stitches could be required, depending on how wide the cables are to be. Some cables are held to the back, some to the front, and still, other cables are made by alternating between holding them to the front and back. Additionally, different patterns may use different abbreviations or will require that you perform an action, like cabling, in a different way than that which you are accustomed, so keep a keen eye out for those differences. Never be afraid to employ your favorite search engine if you come across something with which you are totally unfamiliar. Read each pattern thoroughly and before making that first stitch, make sure you understand what is being asked of you, the knitter.

Chapter 12
Bonus & Conclusion

Hints, Tips, and Reminders

In this section, are listed some helpful hints, tips, and reminders to keep your knitting as worry-free as possible! Your creativity along with your ability is soaring now, but it never hurts to be gently reminded of ways that you can potentially increase your efficiency and decrease your mistakes.

• Always choose yarn that is appropriate to what you are crafting. Give it some thought.

• To knit a looser more open piece you can move up a size or two from what is recommended for your knitting needles. It is advised that you do not move down more than one size from the needles recommended, though.

• When working from a written knitting pattern, before you actually begin any project, be sure to thoroughly read the pattern in its entirety. If you don't understand something or if you encounter unfamiliar techniques or terms, you should look them up and make sure that you understand them before you ever make your cast on row.

• Keep those cast on and bind off rows nice and loose, you do not want any bunched up edges

• When knitting in the round, always check the cast on row and make sure it is not twisted before performing the join.

• Every so often, count your stitches. Even very experienced knitters drop stitches on occasion, and it is much better to catch them sooner than later.

• If you are not happy with a piece when it is finished, try blocking it. If you still are not happy with it, rip it back and start fresh! All great knitters have done it at some point!

- Before blocking, refer to the care instructions given on the ball band of the yarn used for a particular project and always double check before blocking the yarns labeled as blends.

- When you are employing a new stitch or a new technique, take the time to familiarize yourself with how it should look. Examine the stitches closely. This can save you later because you will be able to identify mistakes very quickly and you will give yourself a chance to correct them before they get out of hand.

- Have fun and do try to enjoy your time spent knitting. Try not to bog yourself down too often with deadlines for your projects if you can help it. There is much to be gained by knitting in a relaxed way.

In Closing

Surely by this time in your knitting adventures, you have developed the love for knitting that will see you through many, many more projects. The anticipation of starting a new piece, the sense of pride and confidence in your ability to craft your work, and the feeling of accomplishment upon completion: these are the things that keep us knitters going. Most likely by now you know how good it feels to give a gift that you have crafted with your own two hands and you have received the heartfelt appreciation that comes back to you from the lucky recipient of your handmade gift. Making things is absolutely great but, these, my fellow knitter, are the truly beautiful rewards that you earn as a craftsperson!

Well wishes to you in all of your continued knitting adventures!

Enjoy Knitting!

Elizabeth Hamilton

PD: One more thing. I'd like to give you a gift. If you enjoy knitting as much as I do, you'll probably will love crochet too. So In the next section you will find a preview of my "**CROCHET CRASH COURSE** - The Ultimate Beginner's Course to Learning How to Crochet In Under 12 Hours   Including Quick Projects & Detailed Images".

I know you'll love it!

You can find it on Amazon, under my name, *Elizabeth Hamilton*, or by following this link:

http://www.amazon.com/Crochet-Ultimate-Beginners-Learning-Including-ebook/dp/B00VUDF8BM

Preview of CROCHET CRASH COURSE - The Ultimate Beginner's Course to Learning How to Crochet In Under 12 Hours - *Including Quick Projects & Detailed Images*

Introduction
Welcome to the Amazing World of Crochet!

Welcome to the rich and exhilarating world of crochet! And congratulations for deciding to learn it. That is an excellent choice. This amazing, addictive craft will soon fill your life with joy and colors, with creativity and exhilaration. Crochet lifts up your spirits, helps you relax after a long day and gives you a boost of self-esteem. Yes, it *is* that therapeutic! And there are no words to convey the sheer magic of seeing an object come to life between your fingers, of turning a ball of luscious yarn into a warm and cozy scarf for a loved one, or into a tiny garment for the new baby in your life. You will soon discover that no, you can never have too much yarn in your stash, and that handmade presents say "I love you" better than anything else.

Crochet is a very versatile craft. The possibilities are almost endless, ranging from pretty jewels to full-blown cardigans... and beyond! If some creations, like granny square afghans, do take patience and time, crochet is nonetheless perfect for the impatient as it works up very fast. It takes almost no room in your purse so you can carry it around very easily, which makes it great for "darn, I-forgot-Molly's-birthday!" last-minute gifts. Progress is very quick and sooner than you think, you will be able to finish not-so-small projects over the week-end. Crochet is also, incidentally, quite simple to learn, and you can start making nice items with only a few basic stitches and techniques under your belt. You will soon see that for yourself.

Meant both as a step-by-step introduction to crochet and as a reference tool, this guide will help you get your foot on the ladder and hopefully avoid most of the usual beginner's mistakes.

You will learn how to select your tools; your hook might well become a new best friend of yours, so it is important to choose it carefully. Picking a good yarn is also crucial in many ways. Some crocheters and knitters confess to having a hard time finishing their projects when they do not like the yarn they are using. And that makes sense; after all, crochet is a matter of alchemy between your hook, your yarn, and you. You will also learn that yarns are not interchangeable, that their fiber content affects the way they "behave" and that some yarns are better adapted to certain projects than others.

With that knowledge, and the basic crochet stitches and techniques we will see together, you can make almost everything you want and you will, incidentally, put your new knowledge to good use with fun and easy projects.

Perhaps, when the time comes, you feel confident enough to take the plunge and try your hand (or rather, your crochet hook) at making garments. We will give you a few keys to help you stack all the odds in your favor while teaching you some essential techniques to give your work a professional look and finish.

And then you will be ready to take your first steps alone on the path of your new life, a life we hope will be filled with projects, new techniques, new stitches, tons of yarns and hours of bliss.

* * *

The explanations are given for right-handers, in American English terms. You will find a list of British English equivalents (stitches and crochet hook sizes) at the end of this guide.

For your first steps, we recommend you pick the simplest medium size yarn you can find, in 2 or 3 complementary colors you like, except for black or white, which make the stitches more difficult to see. Stay away from novelty yarn, which proves confusing for beginners as the stitches are lost in the frills. You will also need a crochet hook to go with the yarn. The best choices range from I-9 to K-10 ½ (U.S. size) aka 5.5 to 6.5 mm in metric size. You will also need yarn needles and other small tools. You will find a list in the following pages.

Are you ready for a life-changing journey?

Let's get started!

Part 1
The ABCs of crochet

Before we begin, it is important you should acquaint yourself with the basic crochet terms. Words like "grip", "yarn over" or "loop" are used throughout this guide, in the specialized press, among the crocheters' community and on their blogs. You will run into them eventually, and hopefully use them yourself. You are probably eager to try your crochet hook, but this technical part is the foundation of your new knowledge. See it as a new language you need to learn in order to communicate with other speakers.

First thing first:

Chapter 1
Let's get started!

What is crochet?

Crochet is the art of making fabrics by drawing loops (of thread, or yarn) through other loops by means of a hook. So, the basic starter kit consists in a hook and some yarn. You will also need:

- Small scissors

- A measuring tape

- Yarn needles
  To weave in the ends. Buy them in 2 or 3 different sizes to fit various weights of yarn.

- Stitch markers
  Essential when working in the round. Also very useful to single out a stitch in your work.

The different parts of the crochet hook

Here is the strange, hooked instrument you're going to tame:

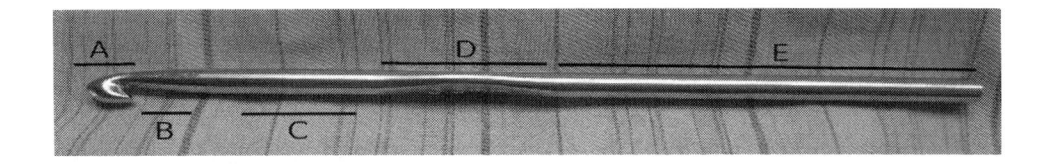

A – The head or point, sometimes also called hook, is the part used to catch the yarn and form stitches.

B – The throat is actually where the stitch is formed.
C – The shaft serves as a "stitch-shaper", giving the stitch its diameter before it is pulled toward the throat to be worked.

D – The grip, or thumb rest, is where, as its name indicates, your thumb is supposed to rest.

E – The handle.

Materials

Crochet hooks come in many different materials. Each has its advantages and its drawbacks. There is no universally ideal crochet hook. You need to try different materials and see for yourself which one you feel the most comfortable with.

- Aluminum / metal

    o Come with or without a handle.

    o **Pros:** Inexpensive, durable, they are available in large ranges of sizes and make a perfect starter kit. They are smooth and thus allow for quick crocheting.

    o **Cons:** Beware of overly cheap handleless models: the paint may chip and get caught in your work. The drawback of their smoothness is that loops sometimes slide off the hook while you are making a stitch. Some people also complain of cramps and pain in the hand when working too long with handleless metal hooks. That is because they unconsciously hold them too tight.

- - Ergonomic crochet hooks are the best compromise. The metal "grips" the yarn and the curves of the handle do not hurt your hand.

- Bamboo

  - **Pros:** Lightweight, flexible, warm in the hand, durable; the more you use them, the smoother they become.

  - **Cons:** Range from 2.5 (B1) to 10 (Q) millimeters only. Stay away from overly cheap crochet hooks: smaller sizes can break when working a tight stitch. Their finish is often far from satisfactory, too, so there might be splinters on the handle. Not only can they split and snag your yarn, they might hurt your hand as well.

- Plastic

  - Come in a large range of sizes and colors.

  - **Pros:** lightweight, smooth, cheap.

  - **Cons:** fragile.

- Wood

  - **Pros:** rather strong and durable. Balanced. Smooth, beautiful.

  - **Cons:** see the drawbacks of smooth, handleless crochet hooks. Some people also complain about blisters because of the high friction inherent to the material.

- Bone

  - Durable and smooth, but no very common.

- Steel

- o   Very strong and durable, but generally used to work lace thread, not yarn. They range from 0.75 (U.S. size 14) to 3.50 (U.S. size 00) millimeters.

- Tunisian (or Afghan) crochet hooks

    - o   Tunisian crochets hooks are different, as the technique of Tunisian crochet is different from the one we are going to learn. You will discover more about that in the Advanced techniques section of this guide.

    - o   The crochet hooks are long, uniform in shape. There is a stopper at one end to prevent the loops from falling off the hook.

    - o   Double-ended versions exist; they have hooks on both ends.

Sizes

Determined by the diameter of its shaft, the size of a crochet hook is written on the thumb rest, or on the handle. It is usually presented as a letter (U.S. system) and / or a number in millimeters (metric system). The smaller the number – the lower the letter in the alphabet – the smaller the crochet hook.

Hooks generally range from 2 millimeters (no U.S. equivalent) to 19 millimeters (U.S. size S).

The measuring system of steel hooks works "in reverse": the higher the number, the smaller the hook.

Important thing to remember: the material of the crochet hook affects the size of your stitch. Let us say you start crocheting a piece with your metal G hook. Then you fall in love with another project and of course, you need to start it right away (welcome to the magical world of UFOs [Unfinished Objects] and WIPs [Works-in-progress]!). But since it calls for a G hook, you have no qualms about "borrowing" it. Later, when you excavate your first project (or, in the jargon, "bring it out of hibernation") and still need a G hook to finish it, you decide to continue with the wooden G hook of the beautiful set auntie Millie has gotten you for Christmas. And that is when you realize that they may both be G sizes, your stitches do not look the same. That is because wooden G hooks are and will always be slightly thicker than metal G hooks. That may not show to the naked eye, but your yarn knows it.

As we will shortly see, yarn manufacturers recommend certain hook sizes to work their yarns. Do not take those recommendations too literally. You can technically use whatever hook size you want with whatever yarn you fancy, *provided* the hook can still catch the yarn and you can pull through easily and smoothly. Using big size hooks with fine yarn will accentuate the openwork effect, while using smaller hooks with thicker yarn will give you a stiffer fabric, perfect for making baskets for instance.

You can find it on Amazon, under my name, *Elizabeth Hamilton*, or by following this link:

http://www.amazon.com/Crochet-Ultimate-Beginners-Learning-Including-ebook/dp/B00VUDF8BM

About the Author

Elizabeth Hamilton had a happy childhood. She learned from her mother all the secrets to become an excellent crafter in the world of needles. Everything started in a comfortable couch in her parents' house living room. That's where the magic started. Very soon Elizabeth realized that her skills were higher than her mother's. Elizabeth knew that with so little you can create so much. Her projects decorated her friends' and relatives' homes.

Many years of practice and studies made her an expert in crochet, knitting, sewing and many other different crafts. During her life she taught and helped a lot of people interested in learning something new and really funny. Neighbors and friends were her first disciples in this wonderful world of crafting

When her first little girl was born, the story repeated. Elizabeth taught her child. Since then Elizabeth understood that perfection is only reachable sharing knowledge. That's why she started to write her book series about Crochet, Knitting, Sewing and many others crafts. These books are written with the same passion and love with which Elizabeth taught her child, relatives, friends and neighbors.

Elizabeth understands the most important problems that people face when they want to start crafting. That's why she knows how to solve them and she provides all the tools, tips and tricks to lead anyone to do magic with needles.